C000063967

From Bonham to Buddha and Back

The Slow Enlightenment Of The
Hard Rock Drummer

Clementine Moss

From Bonham to Buddha and Back:
The Slow Enlightenment of the Hard Rock Drummer
Clementine Moss

Copyright © 2022 by Zepparella Inc.

All rights reserved. No part of this book may be reproduced, stored in a retrieval system, or transmitted in any form by any means electronic or mechanical, including photocopying, recording, or otherwise, except for brief extracts for the purpose of review, without the explicit permission of Clementine Moss and Zepparella Inc.

Zepparella Inc.
San Francisco, California

First Edition

ISBN 979-8-9869789-4-9 – paperback
ISBN 979-8-9869789-5-6 – hard cover
ISBN 979-8-9869789-2-5 – ebook
ISBN 979-8-9869789-3-2 – audio

Cover Art and Design by
Geoff Peveto, thedecoderring.com

Book design by
Tamian Wood, BeyondDesignBooks.com

Back cover photo by Renee Jahnke, reneejahphotography.com

To my teachers, to my father, and to the Old Man, with love.

The dog trots freely in the street
and has his own dog's life to live
and to think about
and to reflect upon
touching and tasting and testing everything
investigating everything
without benefit of perjury
a real realist
with a real tale to tell
and a real tail to tell it with
a real live
    barking
      democratic dog
engaged in real
    free enterprise
with something to say
      about ontology
something to say
      about reality
         and how to see it
            and how to hear it

with his head cocked sideways
at streetcorners
as if he is just about to have
his picture taken
for Victor Records
listening for
His Master's Voice
and looking
like a living questionmark
into the
great gramaphone
of puzzling existence
with its wondrous hollow horn
which always seems
just about to spout forth
some Victorious answer
to everything

~Lawrence Ferlinghetti, "Dog,"
A Coney Island of the Mind: Poems

WHEN THE LEVEE BREAKS

Please listen to the hi-hat on the recorded version of Led Zeppelin's "When the Levee Breaks."

Listen through once. Allow yourself to be transported back to the time or place when you first fell deeply into that trance of sound, so wide and powerful it gave a new depth to your life, a depth you had not known to search for.

Or maybe this is the first time you are hearing the song. In that case, I imagine you prefer different music altogether. Maybe you discount rock and roll as ego-driven, disconnected from that channeled light of Bach or Satie or Django or Monk. No matter. Allow the resistance to rise here as well, then wait for the moment the song breaks through, rings that same truth, that same transportive bell of beauty, that hypnotic atmosphere music offers.

How beautiful to find lessons in our resistance. This may be a foundation of spiritual practice, to dive into the center of no and investigate. All those pronouncements and walls dissolve like so much dust under the microscope of mind.

The trance of song—loud, immense, gorgeous—does the same.

Now we come back to the beginning and start again, this time focusing on the hi-hat. The hi-hat is the pulse at the high end of your hearing. Maybe you've never listened to music closely enough to dissect the sounds of the individual instruments. It may be a sign of a true music lover that you have never zeroed in like that. Maybe the wide view is where enchantment lies. Maybe there is fear in dismantling a big picture into its parts. Maybe the unexamined life is indeed an easier way of living. Would I love a Francis Bacon painting less should I have had any training in brushstrokes and perspective?

We're safe here. As a child, my small periwinkle-colored room was a bass trap. I woke weekend mornings to the sound of my father's stereo cranked up, the bass guitar bleeding through the walls: Beatles, Stones, The Band. I would lie there wondering, trying to figure out the song by its dark clue. Maybe this is why I play drums. My first love was listening to the bass. Maybe from that early training in distinguishing the separate musical voices that make up a song a desire for conversation arose.

Even though I have been listening this way since my suburban California childhood, I can still zoom out and forget specificity. There are many times when I let the song take over and I hear the whole. In fact, when playing drums onstage, this is the ultimate goal.

The enterprise of close listening will not ruin enjoyment; in fact it may offer a kind of deeper appreciation for the song. We learn to parse language and then forget and hear the story. Maybe those who understand the craft of constructing the sentences get to add to their enjoyment the appreciation of *how* the story is told.

Back to the hi-hat. At the top of the song, you hear the drums soloed in a cavern of sound. Here, pick up that pulse of the cymbals, focus your hearing on that frequency as the song roars into being.

In this pulse is the swish of John Bonham's swing. Notice how it rises and falls, louder and softer. Notice how it has its own pattern, its own subtle melody countering and dialoguing with everything else. Notice the perfect placement in time of each swish.

I know it's hard to pay attention straight through, because the harp is so ecstatic, and the guitar paints images, and the bass guitar creates a moving planet on which the whole thing sits. Your internal hearing follows the hi-hat, then gets called to another voice, or to the entirety of sound, and you get lost in the magic.

But then, gently, kindly, come back to that hi-hat pulse, that swing. Here is that subtle something that makes Bonham the greatest rock drummer, that something which is so impossible to replicate. In the conversation between right hand and left foot, stick tip dancing on metal, thunderclap generated by ankle, impossibly small movement creates a world of magic and turns something on in you that you may have never really, *really* turned on.

As the song plays, some light of perfection takes you into a space where thoughts stop. The tension you travel through is desire, longing for the inevitability of explosion into something even more present. Wait for it, all the while inviting the exquisite feeling of anticipation into your bones.

As I play, I become a machine. Not in the "plays like a computer" way a machine is understood these days but in the "transforming into an instrument for sound to travel through" way. There are hooks and pulleys working through my core that follow a program set when Bonham hit the drums in a Headley Grange stairwell a lifetime ago.

In every way my life has turned, this song has met me. As an unhappy teen, a hint of salvation. As a young adult, a connection to sex and power. As a seeking soul in New York City, a call. As a drummer in a stonerrock band living in a van with two other women, a foundation.

Now, I am a drummer in a Led Zeppelin band. The song owns me. I have little say in how I play. Inside this song lives the glory of sublime surrender.

I choose to play a single kick drum on the first beat in the main riff of the song. What you hear on that original recording is a kick drum beat placed ever so perfectly in space, and its echo, like an afterthought, tumbling right after. The echo was created in the reverberation of the stairwell in the light of an afternoon, coupled with a piece of electronic equipment manifesting the delayed beat.

When I choose to play what Bonham played, I play one single kick drum that leaves an empty space for that ghost note, not an imitation of the final product. This choice is not up to me. The song should be played the way Bonham played it. Only then can I land on that first beat of the measure as if I'm leaning on it and pushing off, into the pivoting motion that creates the snare beat. Only then am I aligned with truth.

The decision to play the song this way subjects me to a lot of male opinions, plenty of discussion about how I'm playing it wrong. I guess at some point, I might have cared about that. Here is a moment when the fact that I didn't start playing drums until I was twenty-seven years old seems an enormous stroke of good fortune. My teen self, so full of self-doubt, might have altered her stance and given in to the court of blowhards. Or maybe, if she was playing drums then, she would have stood firmer than I do now. There was a moment back then she could have chosen drums. She wasn't strong enough to do so. I guess she had to move through years of self-doubt before drumming came into her life in order to experience the slow appreciation of her own power.

Back into the verse. Listen to, *feel* the kick drum. Bonham holds back the first beat of each measure, restraining the inevitable freight train drive to the explosion that is the drum-fill funhouse to come. To hold back like that requires restraint, a tightening through my ribcage. I am made of pistons, dependent on air and precision. Air provides steady, lightened energy, and focus keeps me in the moment. I must sit up straight, my arms and legs moving in a surprisingly rigid, squared-off dance. I teeter on a balance of time and space.

The hi-hat. How does it settle with the bass guitar and the bass drum? Notice how you can keep both the lowest sounds and upper sounds in your awareness at the same time. This is the framework, the far edges of the span of song. Circle your attention, high, low, back again, from the hat to the foot, to the bass, circle back to the hat. Fall into the center of this spinning awareness, the center of the song. No matter what melodies drift through, voice and guitar and harp, no matter what thoughts call attention away, the structure provides safety, something to return to. The hi-hat leads us to stillness.

Sound leads us to stillness.

Eventually, the moment of detonation and liberation arrives. Then, the series of fireworks making up the ending vamp. I hit the drums hard through this part. I remember that this song is about a levee, letting loose, and the chaos and racket that comes with letting go. My sticks swing way back, my foot stomps, and my ankle creates trilling, rumbling fills with the ball of my foot. All along, there is that swing on the hat.

Through the outro, my hand crashes down on the hi-hat cymbals that are now wide open, a gruesome, relentless swing. The last hit sends the song into the universe, traveling back to the bang that started it all. It's over. The long breath that follows is forlorn, and I already long for the next time.

2

The house exists only in memory. Smell of salt and sea, shade of midday. Nothing of street or sky, just a path to green lawn. Hard, warm concrete yields to soft clover, cradling my feet.

I toddle across the lawn. My legs are unsteadiness and resolve. A bird-of-paradise flies at the far edge and I'm pulled there. The flower bends level to my crown: brilliant orange, yellow, a stripe of red along the rippled edges. I hold it, slick and weighty in my two hands. I tilt the tip of the petals toward my mouth.

A kind of honeysuckle rolls onto my tongue and down my throat. Warm, bright, radiant light tumbles like flavor into me, finds exit through my pores and fingertips. Sweet liquid falls in, and then light shoots out through any place it can find. What a funny, bright light this is. How far it shoots out of every place it can find. I hold up my hands to see.

I know the bliss of a star.

My name is called. The light shuts off. I set the flower back to nodding in air and again, cool grass on my feet as I turn toward the house.

❧

I didn't expect this. A hard rock drummer, and strange.

Maybe I've wasted my whole life sleepwalking, no plan, baffled and batted around by impulses, by my mind, my thoughts, my fear. Thinking if I tasted everything offered I would find that light again.

Strange, because it doesn't seem like a waste.

I have a rent-controlled apartment, a daily meditation practice, three bands, three drum sets, and a studio that is cluttered and dusty and contains all I own of value.

I'm broke. I'm pissed off my jeans don't fit.

I go for weeks, a month, so pure I have no use for deodorant: only raw foods and the right number of steps and Pilates and colonics and on and on. Every new and life-prolonging Whole Foods sniffing action—I'm on it.

I meditate in the morning, bringing myself into my heart center, and become peace.

Later that night I trade ten dollars for a smoke from a bunch of heroin addicts in the park playing Grateful Dead songs and nursing their pit bull puppies. Grateful Dead *song*, the same first measure, over and over.

I drink matcha tea in the morning and put in a little bit of coconut oil so I don't get overloaded with the caffeine boost.

I drive eleven hours to a show in Portland with Red Bull and Power Bars as fuel.

I aim to tear into the drums like a gorilla, epically huge and powerful behind the kit. After the show, I collapse in self-loathing when I see the gorilla come to life in a fan photo on Facebook.

I see beauty in the humans I encounter, forever opening to the godliness at the center of each being. Meanwhile, a mantra of self-loathing animates my every step.

Back and forth I go.

The thing is, there is still that bird-of-paradise.

The first book I read about Buddhism was *The Three Pillars of Zen*. I got stuck on one concept, and it bothered me endlessly.

How can the loss of the self equal happiness if what I do and whom I love is what makes me happy? How can drumming make me so happy yet represent an attachment to the self I am to let go?

I was at a ten-day meditation retreat in the golden plains west of Dallas, and it was the seventh day. The center of my being expanded, and my pores opened. I started breathing out of my skin, becoming more and more insubstantial. A bird outside the window sang a song, and the song blew through me like a breeze. The self fell away. Only bliss was there.

If I could say I lived in that space always, I would be a Buddha. I would have come home to the light of that honeysuckle.

Instead, I'm a rock-and-roll drummer. Those few seconds of awareness shine like a small pinprick of light on a dark and noisy stage.

3 Within the drum is a voice.

The voice speaks stories as I strum and caress and play. My fingertips play. I can't bear to allow the beater and stick to make contact. The elk skin stretched over the frame demands the touch of my skin, the slight catch of my fingerprint against the cool of the drumhead. I want nothing between me and that glorious moment when my finger moves toward the center of the drum and finds bounce and reverberation.

The sound rises out of the drum and resonates in the tips of my fingers, up through body to heart. The heart is a drum that vibrates. It is heart to drum and drum to drum. The heart of the planet is the same frequency as the drum. It is heart to heart and drum to drum through the touch of my fingertips.

Fingertips bitten to the quick, an old habit. Before there was the drum there were habits, and sometimes I list into these old patterns. I am pulled to memories and energetic patterns that rise, magnetic symbols forming from the dust of this body. The drum speaks. Even the nail-biting is divine.

Here is the most shocking thing I could say at this late age.

As I drum, I know myself and all things as God.

As I drum, I know the divine.

The drum is primary language, the first note sung, *Om* vibrating here, from this stretched skin so resonant. The strangest thing to happen in my love affair with the drum is that my surrender should be so complete, this surrender to divine will. The drum has brought me here.

In fact, drums brought me everywhere I was meant to be. Through the grime of cities and the landscapes of interstates. Into love affairs and beds and near addictions. Drunken nights of after-show parties, shoes sticky on theater floors as we danced and stumbled and air-guitared to our favorite songs—glorious moments in the life of a touring musician.

Then into self-exploration.

And finally, to God.

I don't say that lightly. I still cringe when the word is spoken. Yet this union with the divine is so apparent when the drum speaks within and through. My mind fills with light and no-thought space. I play the drum and truth rings. Only now have I learned to listen.

Believe me when I say I have a desire to create something shocking in these pages. I wrestle to come up with something that would be pleasing to the human sense of drama: intrigue or gossip or horror or torture. Believe me when I tell you that none of that could be more shocking than this development, this devotion. This is the most shocking, the most offensive, the most open to ridicule, the most grating thing I could say.

The drum teaches me to know all things as God.

The thing about the drum is there is silence within it. Within each drumbeat, within our hearts as well, moments of silence allow us to hang suspended in divinity, between beats. When we practice meditation or breathing exercises, what we are looking for is the silence there. It is the same with the drum.

The vast, dark stillness of unknown space between beats is the most terrifying of all things.

The silence in the heart is what we run from. Silence is so moving, so vulnerable, so devotional. Will there be another beat, a continuation? We shudder at our sweet dependence on the unseen force that drives toward or away from the next pulse. When we live in the silence, we surrender. We give up our will. And the giving up, against which we fight endlessly, makes for those stories we crave.

The recognition of silence within ourselves, and thus each other, is what we seek. We surrender within ourselves and then recognize this silence in all heartbeats. Once we get a taste for silence, it becomes harder to prop up the personality structure that hides this delicate stillness from the world in a dire exercise of will. We are born to build a cage to hide this primordial and exquisite secret. The cage dissolves as the stillness takes over.

My cage gets rattled open by sound and vibration. The drum and I are one.

(A stage manager said that to me once, as I left the stage after a show. *You are one with the drums.* I stood there, streaked with sweat, trying to catch my breath, the set ringing in my ears, every bit of energy wrung out of me.)

The slide guitar begins.

The story begins to call. The sound of the drum announces the tale. Why should I write of music, except that it is vibration, universal love, longing and magic rising from strings and snares and resonant heads. I speak of silence here, and all great music understands that silence is yet another voice.

In writing, I fail before I begin. Isn't there some kind of darkness I am to tell about? The lifelong struggle with the physical body, or the up and the down of mental depression, anguish, heartbreak, or the rock-and-roll excursions into sex and drugs, the decay. I moved through it all, am moving still. The story was dirty and at times despairing but no better or worse than anyone's story, and therefore, it was the story of life, of every life: hiding from silence, holding on desperately to the illusion of being not worthy of divine light.

I didn't feel I was enough. Isn't that our deepest struggle, feeling not enough? Yet this goes with the territory, since it is true. We are not enough. The personality self knows this. The personality self will never be enough as long as it believes it is separate from the divine. On that single mis-knowing rests the endless, tired saga of agony on which stories sit.

When I say "the divine" you may think of your own God and or some imposed God. It is of no consequence how you assign it. We get caught up in semantics, but really what I mean is the energy holding molecules in place. Consciousness. Love. Mystery. Nature. Power. Intent. The single thought that manifests all being into existence. Most believe the divine to be separate from themselves. How could anything be outside of the eternal whole? The personality self is never enough, although in a cosmic joke, it too is just as divine as any of it. Nothing is outside of God.

I say the word God because I still, after all these years, feel the rise I get from the word, the twinge of horror. Here is where you meet the one raised on rock and roll, the one idolizing those who get a rise, who disrupt. Who knew that the most outlaw thing I could say would be hiding in this word?

(I remember sitting in a high school classroom in the 1980s, the born-again Christian girl trying to engage me with a conversation about Christian rock. The blasphemy I felt, the corruption of the truly holy . . .)

The slide guitar begins.

The drum tells stories, and the stories meet the vibration of the heart and dissolve in the single note of the one song endlessly playing.

Most of my spiritual practice has been a struggle to let go of the attachment to story. This is Buddhism 101, releasing of attachments, cravings, aversions. This is Shamanism, traveling by boat to retrieve soul parts left behind during times of trauma, taking back our stories and our pain to integrate and release them. We let go of suffering by sacrificing its energy to the frequency of the drum.

How to write a parable of letting go of suffering when the attachment to story is the suffering?

There is so little suffering here for me now, but lack of suffering can't possibly be the story, can it? This can't be a story of how I let go of suffering, since it is only in letting go of the storyteller that suffering ends. Even the story is divine, the heart of the storyteller with it.

The slide guitar begins.

Still, I hear another tale, insistently making its way to these pages. Maybe the pieces will make up the whole, the individual voices creating a picture, a wider view that I may look at and hear. The drum will tell the stories, since its voice loves to do so, and love bends all to its purpose. I sink into silence while the stories rise. I long for them to resonate with the heart of the world, and meet your own.

The slide guitar begins.
It fills the monitor and fills the stage and fills the venue and it fills me up, hitting the frequency of my being.

My back straightens, and I settle solidly on the drum stool. My hips are right angles. My feet melt into the pedals.

I breathe deeply, drawing the smell of bodies and heated amplifier tubes and drink-soaked carpets and beer taps and electricity into my lungs, and I rest, unclenching my chest muscles and shoulders. The air runs down my center and into my diaphragm.

My pores expand, and sound enters, vibrating the channels in my veins open, widening tracks around my veins as they travel through muscle and tissue.

I become a cavity for sound, and nothing touches anything.

The sticks lie on the snare drum, and my hands rest lightly on my thighs. I don't feel them. Behind my eyelids, round shapes trail colors across my vision, reflections of the lights above.

As my head tilts, the light becomes white. White light and sound become my reality. My mind is as porous as my body.

Sound passes through me as a wind through grass. Though so far tonight, on this stage, I have been a piece of machinery conveying the music, now the music carries me.

My shoulders fill, my back broadens, the light gets whiter, hotter, and my head drops slightly and starts moving from side to side, ears sweeping back and forth to gather more of the sound. Power expands my core, and now, with an electric shiver, everything in the body feels. All sensation comes alive and awareness sweeps in waves through form.

The sticks are in my hand, and the cue is coming.

My eyes race back and forth behind their lids. Colors flash and awareness of feeling leaps around: the stick on my first finger, my forearm resting on my leg, my feet heavy on the pedals, the heat at the top of my head, and above all, the breath, the breath traveling to the deepest part of my center and radiating out along its path.

I hit the first crash cymbal and lock into the pattern. I am not me. My body plays with a power and connection to the sound. I feel the strength of my upper arms in a dreaming, detached way. The tree trunk of my back sways. This is not my body. It is so strong, and quick flashes of worry that the strength will end spark like fireflies. I observe, aware only of slide guitar in nothingness. When the measures end and the band stops for the first interlude, a radiant joy, not from me but from inside the slide guitar, fills all space in the universe.

The body begins again.

I need to open my eyes to catch the cue. That eventuality bears down on me, and my mind floats back to the room. A ripple of dread tracks through my skin. I want to keep my eyes closed and my mind empty and my body taken over by the unknown spirit that plays the drums, but I need to catch the cue from the guitarist. I am unsteady between two realities. In this reality, I'm only a mechanism of the slide guitar. In that reality, the guitarist is turning around, lifting the guitar, cueing me for the abrupt stop.

I come rushing back. With my own mind, my own body, my own doubts and inabilities, the song continues. I am required to think and count and remember.

As the last note rings out, whatever spirit or entity that has been playing the drums is gone. I open my eyes, and the lights, with their small halos, black out the audience. The air seems thin. I lean over to pick up my water bottle off the ground before the next song. I chide myself behind the protective curtain of blonde hair.

You're such a hippie!

I shake my head slightly. At the edge of my vision, I see someone standing on the corner of the stage. My heart leaps for a moment, until I see it is a curtain on a microphone stand. I am always seeing ghosts in rock clubs, usually my dad. No matter how many years go by, I will always be sad he never saw me play. He died at the age of fifty-four, a couple of years after I started taking drum lessons. He was the ultimate music fan. Every time my family sees me play, someone says, "Dad would have loved this."

The guitarist steps toward me and wipes her guitar with a towel. She gives me a smile. I have an interior conversation with her. I hear her tease me. *Dude! Too many trips around the universe, you think? As long as you're channeling spirits, why don't you see if you can conjure up Mozart for me. Or, hell, what about Django?* She steps to her pedalboard, oblivious to my train of thought.

Okay. A peace settles on me. As we launch into the next song, I joyfully bash my critical mind into silence. Let me be a channel. I don't care how it would sound to say it. I'm open. Let the bass line carry spirits along my own little river of blood. My wrists are so loose, and I'm barely holding the sticks as they bounce off the drumheads.

The chorus hits, and I am lying on the carpeted floor of a beat-up van hurtling to a barter festival in 1987. It's pitch dark, and I know people around me are talking and laughing, but all I can hear is Led Zeppelin, so loud I'm on my own rolling planet of sound. *If this is the way I go, so be it.* A rumbling chaotic cocoon of music speeding into the night, "Immigrant Song" carrying me into fearless space.

My mind splays out on the drum set like I tripped over a curb. The solo section! Eyes open, sharply aware, the critic rushes in. The lights are hot and the monitor feeds back and interior dialogue shouts a tirade.

Goddamn it! If you would fucking practice you would know what the hell to do in this part!

I come out of a drum fill in a jerky, ridiculous way. The guitarist looks back and gives me a surprised look that says, *Hey! Hold it together!*

I reach for patterns that don't make sense. I yell out, trying to draw myself back into the flow, into the cocoon, but it's gone. I crab at myself for the rest of the song.

Terrible, terrible drummer! Fraud!

I could crawl off the drum throne and hide behind the bass rig.

Had to be a drummer. Couldn't be a front person and be able to get drunk and excused. Yet another case of the limited thinking that's informed your whole fucking life.

I pull jagged breaths into my throat and can't remember how it feels to breathe deeply. I try to get back to anywhere else I've been tonight, but I look at my drums and the equipment seems off. The seat is too high, the snare too low, the ride cymbal tilted weird. It's a wonder I can play at all.

On top of that, the stage is fucking hot. My hands have trouble holding on to the sticks, and I remember a drummer who spent time sanding his down before every show. I shouldn't have made fun of him. *Who's laughing now, asshole?* I concentrate on keeping the sticks in my hands and a blister has formed. The singer's milking the outros a little more than usual tonight, and that pisses me off too. I disappear into a pocket of rage and assault the drums until my thoughts speak only transcription.

Out of the guitar solo into the drum fill: lead with the right hand, snare, then tom, head into the last verse, fall through time, adjust the push into pull, back and back and back. Hit that last fill . . . lead with the left on that one, don't mess it up, wait until it builds right until you finish. INTENTION. Redeem yourself here, jackass. Crash. Done. Put your head down and disappear, you hack of a human being.

A guitar change. I lean down for more water and wipe the hair off my face. I check the hi-hat clutch and look around, glare fiercely at how everything is positioned, then closing my eyes and straightening my back, I let it go.

Just let it go.

I rub my hands on my pants, turning them over to dry a little, and breathe, long breaths that I draw into my diaphragm and release. I wonder if anyone ever notices me struggling to settle my breath. *Don't force, just observe.*

The breaths come easier, and the room fades away.

The slide guitar begins.

My head tilts toward the lights and my breath radiates to the tips of my fingers and runs the length of my body, opening every muscle like water running over a stone path. Music fills me. The light behind my eyes ignites.

The song starts, and I am not the one who plays. These are not my hands striking the drums, the cymbals. That is not my foot on the pedal. My shoulders are wide and strong, and a spark runs to every corner of my body in a glory of sensation: the wood against my knuckle, the vinyl seat on the back of my thighs, the taste of electricity at the back of my throat, the ache in my neck, and the light, the light that prisms through my mind and combines with the sound of the slide guitar to create a lightning sky.

Tears spout. I see sprinklers on a lawn.

I launch into the pattern, my body leaning behind the beat, and now it is early morning with my father's southern rock blasting us awake. A funny patience passes through me: the image of a father with a child on his feet learning dance steps. I inhabit another body and lead the limbs through the motions.

I smell my father's skin.

The wide, hairy chest, the head of thick black hair, the enormous hands, coarse from years of manual labor, the scratch of his chin, the big belly, that haven of a body. Protection in his powerful arms, drowsy naps on the couch, my feet in his hands. I protected him too, peeling his sunburned skin between the hairs on his arm, walking on top of him to get the kinks out of his back.

Lost in the enveloping sadness of my father's smell, I spin further away.

A flurry of images: sitting on his shoulders, pulling on a chain on a garage door. He's showing me how to dance. *Not like that, listen to the rhythm, like this.* His booming voice, hands pulling me from the water, cradling me in a towel, carrying me to bed, rubbing my back, tagging me out, showing me how.

The boat is in the center of glass, and we float on the pivot of morning, watching the red sunrise off the rocks.

Dad's body, the barrel chest, the arms so strong, the thick legs, the fat, solid feet. I always miss the man, but right now I miss his body, a physical presence I knew intimately as a child knows her parent.

My limbs ache and grow thick and heavy. Beating the drums beats blood into my heart, which is breaking. His blood flies through my veins as the song plays on.

Words spill over the top of my brain like water from a garden hose.

Stay with me, Dad.

I watch words take the path of my breath to the tips of my fingers.

Stay with me.

Words I never got to say pour over my tongue.

Stay with me, it's okay, just stay with me.

I repeat it over and over as I feel him fading away. It becomes a part of the rhythm I play, a mantra that drives the tempo of the song.

Daddy. Dad. Don't leave. Stay with me.

My eyes open. He's gone in that second. I choke on the emptiness and hit the cymbal with an arm weighted with sorrow. I am alone onstage and see no one. I look into the lights above and try to open that space back up for him. I try to keep my heart bereft.

It works for a time, but the venue is so loud. The sticks slip in my hands, the air is thick, it's difficult to swallow. There's someone in the front row punching the sky. The audience roars in my ears. The vocal sounds pure and strong, and I love the way she sings this part. I love this song.

The band plays on.

Lead with the right on this one, start in triplets and run through the toms with sixteenths. My favorite fill. The guitarist and bass player look back at me as I come in strong to the outro and we share a moment of real connection in this reality, right now. I am wrapped up in love for these songs through the rest of the set and feel happy.

Once, during "Whole Lotta Love," I catch that curtain and microphone stand in the corner of my eye, and for the rest of the song I let it be Dad, rockin' out sidestage the way he would have done.

5 I have a funny relationship with time. As a drummer, time is my job.

I push it, pull it, hang in it, subdivide it. I affect a whole concert by my understanding of it, and this understanding affects everyone in the room. In fact, what you think of me as a drummer is what you think of my time. Whether you see one concert or a handful, the way I sit in time will affect the way you love or hate my playing.

When I am tired, time slows down, so as I play my body speeds up, overcompensating. When my body and mind are aligned, there is a narrow groove in the song into which I settle like a tire in tracks of dried mud. I play best when I can control the downhill speed as deftly as the uphill, when there is no getting out of that groove.

The relationship between the time in my right foot and my hi-hat hand is particular to those two limbs, how they play off each other, how they speak within space. Each limb combination has its own history, its own fraught drama. For years as I played, I begged my left foot to participate in the conversation, and one night, there it was, bouncing on its own, singing its own song and relating to the others as if it were a prodigal son, somehow returned.

When I started playing drums, I realized I saw each beat as a block, hanging in space, relating to the other blocks representing beats played by other limbs. Am I then involved in time, or in space?

How subtle the whisper of time between beats. Subtle, yet for a musician the space between beats can be as wide as an ocean, as meaningful as the difference between a transcendent player and a perfunctory one.

The mind reflects its understanding of time to the listener, and we intuit the mind of the drummer drifting when the time drifts. When every hit of the drum pattern is present and alive, we respond in kind. We pay attention because the drummer is wrapping us in her attention, and we allow ourselves to be carried away. When she is focused, we can fly.

It is apparent when the mind tries to exert control over the moment. If I launch into a pattern with trepidation, or anticipatory fear of a future pattern, if I start to ruminate over the pattern I've just played, then you hear me play as if I'm falling down stairs—and not in a good way. I say, *This is my brain on drums*. But really, it's the future and past getting tangled up in the Now.

Maybe my obsession with time started early, with a father who seemed constantly in a rush to be the first one anywhere. His need to move quickly informed our mornings, so when we woke, we were to be up and going immediately, pleasantly. No luxuriating in trails of dreams or grousing about the rising.

I have to be the first one anywhere too. Where the hell am I trying to go so fast? Do I really want to be first? There is a vivid, funny memory in my mind of sitting in a living room with a group of children. When the adult announced we were going outside to play, I leaped up and ran outside to be first, only to bounce off the sliding glass door and land in the center of seated children. That's me, on a spring, propelled to be first in line no matter the consequences.

In my first Vipassana meditation retreat and the nine-day vow of silence, I was amazed how I lost track of time calibration. I would take a nap and wake in a panic: *I must have been sleeping three hours! I must have missed the sit!* Only to find I had been dozing for twenty minutes. Time stretched out in a way I had never experienced before. I was constantly astounded how wide the experience of time could be, after a lifetime of keeping a narrow vision on the moments in my days.

Eckhart Tolle speaks often of time and what he calls "psychological time."

> *"To be identified with your mind is to be trapped in time: the compulsion to live almost exclusively through memory and anticipation."[1]*

Psychological time is the illusion of time created by the mind. Tolle explains that we are never right here, but forever looking to the past to make sense of our experience, or to the future to anticipate what will happen next. The clarity of the Now was what I was experiencing at the meditation retreat, as the mind began to quiet and let go of its hold on me. I fell into each moment.

For all my love of time and my lifetime exploration of it, when I forget it, I am happiest.

When my father died, I took no comfort in knowing that time soothes grief. I wanted the missing to hurt forever. As the years passed, I took solace in knowing that the missing does not go away but time teaches us to manage the ache. I was happy to discover that time does not heal all wounds, and the enduring pain can transform into a great teacher.

In hospice work, one part of the training is to write down all the things you will have to let go of when terminally ill: your friends, your body, walking down the street, being with trees. This seems like a good lesson, to recognize how much time gives us and how much it takes away.

Or, are all these things, these moments, these loves, these passions, all existing at once, into eternity? Albert Einstein said: "The distinction between the past, present and future is only a stubbornly persistent illusion." In that case, what exists always exists, no matter our perception.

I do take solace in that. Then, I spin out into my days, savoring the gift of moments, and always looking for that groove to carry me away.

6 The van is very comfortable, but no matter who you are, being cooped up for so long can be rough. Ours are often long drives, barreling down highways with infrequent stops.

We time our hydration so we are on the same page with rest stops. Everyone has their little area where they nestle in and work on the computer, read if it's a flat road, and sleep. Sometimes, my bandmates will play their instruments, practicing for an upcoming show or writing.

We listen to music individually, so the van is very quiet most of the time. I know the Hollywood image of a band on the road is of the stereo blasting music nonstop. In reality, with so little personal space, harmony comes when each person gets their alone time, even when only inches away from the others. This is the beauty of headphones.

Of course, there are also hours of long, rambling conversations about pretty much everything. I am the driver, and often a band member will keep me company in the passenger seat. These conversations unravel like the yellow line carrying us along the track of asphalt. Little is unsaid. We sail through wide expanses of earth and sky, letting loose any barriers to free conversation. We expand our ideas and spin out trains of thought that can go for hours. There is time for observation, for every possibility, for imagination. There is time for examining every side of an issue, for making wild suggestions, for diving in deep.

When one person brings up a problem, the others rally together and parse it out, dissect and look at it from every angle.

We have time, so much time for this. Each of these women is thoughtful, smart, and compassionate, and we empathize with problems as if they're our own. This is my tribe, the ones I learn from, the ones I get truth from. Their support is as cushioning as the chassis carrying me through the landscapes of hours.

The first gift is finding someone to play with to whom you like to talk, someone you like to be with. Someone you can stand to hang out with, be with in a hotel room or a crowded car or a stinky backstage room. Someone you can laugh with so hard you have to leave the room to breathe again. Someone who listens to what you are saying musically and who converses with you onstage as well as off.

Someone who listens. Musicians get so wrapped up in their technique, in their instrument, in their mind, that playing with someone who listens to what the rest of the band is doing in the moment is important.

The next gift in a bandmate is in finding someone who has similar musical goals, who wants to put into their career the same amount that you want to put into yours. Finding someone who is as driven as you is the real magic. Finding someone who comes to music with the same degree of love for it, that's all there is. Then, you are always on the same page about what's important. You will work together through the years to keep finding harmony in the details, but you can be confident that you are always together in the big picture.

I have heard it said that to be a great band there must be some friction. I know the stories of musicians who have been in bands for forty years who can't stand their bandmates, and interactions are passive-aggressive dances thwarting each other. I have experienced these relationships in bands, and there is an energy to it. Maybe it makes for a better show, who knows.

Gretchen and I have played music together for many years.

We are more alike than different. I would say time has proven we are perfectly complementary. We are both nerds, autodidactic, readers and writers. I would say she is more verbal than I, but that isn't a far stretch. It would be difficult to find anyone as well-spoken as Gretchen. Her ability to think quickly and speak eloquently makes conversations with her a delight.

Gretchen has a magical ability to see through problems to solutions. This is the second thing people fall in love with. The first is her open, light, and friendly manner, and the fact that she doesn't seem self-conscious about how physically beautiful she is. The way she looks is an entry into her true loveliness.

That is one big difference between us. She is friendlier than I, thoughtful, kind, compassionate. I am more internal, moodier, empathetic to the point of feeling buffeted about by energy. This can cause me to clam up, get cold and grouchy. In groups of people, I get quieter, wanting time in my own head without the bombardment of other people's energies interfering with mine. This is where we're different. She always gives people more than they expect.

At the same time, we are each happy in solitude. We make each other laugh. I think she's a riot, with a dark and juvenile humor that leaves me in stitches.

Musically, she is as present as she is in every other part of her life. A diligent practicer, a constant learner, an inspired composer.

When we started playing together in an AC/DC band, it was her first rock band. I remember standing behind her in the club before our first show, seeing her narrow shoulders silhouetted against the light of the stage. I felt protective immediately. That feeling has never left. Little did I know how much she would be teaching me over the years, about focus and fastidiousness, about never settling for less than what I can imagine, in music and in life.

That last one is a hard lesson for me. I tend toward rapidity over quality. She taught me to slow down and get it right.

When we play music together, her guitar is what I listen to first. I marvel at how intimate this musical conversation has become over time. I can hear the smallest idiosyncrasies in her playing so clearly. Sometimes, by very slight changes in her guitar line, I know we are getting out of sync, or that she needs more support, or that she is trying to pull me back to a more settled pace.

The push and pull of tempo is a constant conversation, sometimes funny, one of us rushing headlong or pulling too far back. She is consistency. I get carried away. This is how we complement each other. She keeps me in check. I keep her guessing.

Most of the time though, we are in sync. In the beginning guitar solo of "Dazed and Confused," there is a tiny exclamation she makes at the end of a phrase that signals me to start the crescendo, like a little buzzing bee she lets fly to alert me. It happens in a split second, and I follow the clue to the heart of the song, to the beauty of speaking in unison.

I can read the sound of her fingers on the strings clearer than I can read her expressions, as she turns back to me to communicate a message mid-song. Sometimes our eyes lock, and we are of the same mind. Sometimes, we comically gesture and then give up the idea of trying to convey a thought in a nonmusical way. Sometimes, I try to let her know how much I love playing a song we have played hundreds of times and how much I love to open my eyes and see her there again.

9

The train tracks lead us to the dirtiest part of town. That's always where the rock club is.

We pull around the back into the alley behind the venue and knock on the metal door. The soundman looks as if he just woke up. He props the door open with a concrete brick. We unlatch the back of the van and start carrying equipment into the dark club, lit only by the stage lights and the afternoon dust coming in through the bars of the front windows. It smells like beer taps and bleach and vaguely of vomit. That may be from the trash bins we pass on the way in that seem to be oozing something milky. Garbage load-in, we say.

It feels good to walk, to lift heavy things after driving. During the year of shows it becomes so second nature, the loading in and loading out. Some nights it happens without me even being aware of doing it. Any load without stairs is heaven.

I set up the drums while the other two position the amps, and while instruments are being mic'd the bass player sets up the merchandise and the guitarist restrings her guitar. I talk to the promoter, or fidget with the drums, or waste a dollar in the pinball machine. We sound check, figure out dinner, clean up a little, and get dressed and put on makeup. I comb out my hair with my fingers.

Then, I sleep. The greenroom is usually behind the stage, so it's deafening in there as the opening bands play. I let the bass frequencies lull me to a deep slumber. My body feels so heavy before I'm set to play, as if it knows what is coming, as if it knows the exertion I'm going to put it through. For the

rest of my life, when I am in a loud room, I get sleepy. I fall
asleep during loud action movies, the opera, the symphony.
Any place where I can sit comfortably and be surrounded by
heavy bass frequencies, I'm toast. Years of this backstage nap
has Pavlov's-dogged me.

Many nights, I step onstage wiping moisture from the
corners of my mouth. The drooling drummer, that sounds
like a joke. The first strikes on the drums clear out the cobwebs, and I arrive.

I am living on the road for a year, in a different city every night. I am playing a kind of heavy rock that lends itself
to power in drumming. Up until this point, my life has been
one of careful self-consciousness. I'm in my early thirties. My
twenties were spent in a sort of self-regarding haze, concerned
with judgment, mine harshest of all.

Each night, I am in nightclubs filled with men. The chicks
who attend are all sisters—there are so few of us. If we have
never played the venue before, the soundman will be condescending to my band before the show. I use my annoyance at
him to fuel my performance. It's great to be underestimated.
Makes me want to hit things even harder, and I do.

Before the show, I walk through the club, purposeful. The
night is mine. I head to the restroom and see my two bandmates there, shaking the day's drive out of their hair. In the
mirror with them I feel strong in triplicate. They are powerful
too, and the three together are magic. As we thread our way
back through the crowd, their light shines on me, and I am
even more settled and strong.

There is a drum set waiting for me. It is the best beauty
accessory I could have. Behind the kit I aim to be huge, a monster. I believe that to really be a player you must embrace the
abandon that happens in the moment. Flying over the drums,

straining to hit it right, throwing it all in to make people feel, make people move. I can't control my facial expressions when I'm really in it. I am distrustful of good-looking drummers and singers who don't sweat. My guitarist bleeds on her guitar. I learn that embracing ugliness is where beauty lies.

IMMIGRANT SONG

10 "Immigrant Song." Increments of time are important here. We widen out and focus in. Funny how much of spiritual practice is about expanding our awareness, and then funny how much of spiritual practice is about focusing narrower and narrower on one particular point. It is the same in drumming.

This song requires one to subdivide moments of space in an exacting way. We must look closely in order for the small fractions of time to push the song forward and to pull the song back. The subtle shift between the two forces creates the swing.

The song is an exploration of relationships. Relationship of time and beats, some precise, some relaxed. Relationship of instruments: bass, drums, guitar. A triangle of those three voices conjures a container in which the vocal dances. The snare drum and the bass drum romp with each other. There must be no hesitation and no rush. The conversation of hi-hat to snare is another affair, holding tight in the center of the protective ring of drums.

The economy of dynamics is here. Perfect restraint, the build to detonation. This is sex in all its marauding, relentless, inevitable energy. The energy of young men with no limit to the taking.

How can we play the songs of these men, culture-indulged twentysomethings singing in a revelry of rampant, indulgent, trouncing power?

As the culture awakens, we peer backward to see how long transgressions have been around. Here is a symbolic point of history on which to focus, 1970s rock and roll, young women as trophies, used and discarded. We know the stories. We follow the winding progression of rule and realize how much has been out of balance, and for so long. How did we not notice or see or care?

As women, we look back and see that while we thought we were free, we were playing right into hands holding power, absorbing values of surrender while thinking we were breaking ground.

This is what it looks like to newly judge behavior in retrospect. I say "newly," because I am of the generation that followed the '70s rock stars, and it took a long time for it to occur to me that the reason the girls I idolized seemed older than their years may have been the result of early trauma. It didn't occur to me that power was being wielded unfairly or cruelly or coldly, that vulnerability was being taken advantage of, and that this advantage was the subtext of songs I loved, and still love.

I was one of the too-young girls who would say she knew exactly what she was doing, choosing sex as power. I would not have believed that my precociousness was anything other than biological. I would have been appalled if it had been suggested that this early sexuality was something cultivated and owned by the culture at large. I had an older boyfriend, not a rock star. I was turned on by the music I was listening to and by Beat writers who wrote of wanderlust and sexual revelry. I longed to be older, to be away from that which made me miserable and feel less than. Sex was all mine, when so much else was to please everyone else.

When I was fourteen years old, I had a boyfriend who lived forty-five minutes from my house. I have no memory of how I met him. We rarely saw each other. He once rode his bicycle twenty-three miles from his house in the Anaheim Hills to my house in El Toro.

Most of the time, our relationship happened on the phone. We would fall asleep sometimes listening to "Down By The Seaside" and "The Rain Song" together, somehow, those dreamy Zeppelin tunes surrounding us in the midnight hours in an inebriation of desire.

Once, I spent an afternoon at his house, right after he got his driver's license. He drove into our cul-de-sac in a beat-up brown muscle car that sounded as though it could die at any time. We entered his home, and I was briefly introduced to his Eastern European mother. He sort of ignored her, and we went up the white carpeted stairs to his room.

We spent a sunlit afternoon on his carpet in a reverie of Led Zeppelin, sealing the exquisite intoxication of skin-to-skin contact into the songs. The tactile overload in this music is what I look for when I close my eyes onstage. I close my eyes to find, to convey, to connect with our collective memory of sweet exploration, that transportive light to which we forever ache to return.

So how to reconcile the music I love and the history that brought it forward?

A dear friend used to say, "Everyone wants a Van Gogh in their living room, but no one wants Van Gogh in their living room." We separate the art from the artist. The staying power of Led Zeppelin songs is that ultimately, they are about love, the power of love. I have understood this firsthand, in fading afternoon light tinged with the exquisite pain of the inevitable return to the prosaic. I get to interpret the songs as I have lived them, and they are mine.

I see power differently now, as a personal power within myself. My power is knowing what aligns with my highest good. I think I knew it even then, and I am a lucky one. We all see power differently, day by day—and day by day, we learn to align to a new understanding.

The men who wrote these songs may be different now, or they may not. I know I am different and come to the songs with eyes open. I widen my vision, then bring it right back to millimeters. In the tension holding the beats lies a universe of ever-deepening understanding.

11

Three hundred twenty shows in one year. We lived in the van.

We didn't care about what anyone thought we were doing or what they thought of us or of our agenda. We weren't driven by a desire to please. The Jiffy Lube guy who traded us an oil change for a joint, he knew as much about us as anyone did. He didn't try to hit on us or treat us with condescension. He knew the ball was in our court. He bowed to the power of three.

We stood together no matter the internal cracks. The best way to get us to play well was to insult us, one or all. In fact, sometimes we'd use that knowledge, the unity of the common enemy, to our own advantage. If we were feeling a little lackadaisical or unconnected before a show, one of us would bring up an old insult while we were getting ready to take the stage, and then we were going to ram the music down every throat in the venue, together.

Each night was different, the guitar unearthing melodies and new rhythms endlessly born, the right foot trying a different pattern, the tempo adjusting, the ear uncovering something new.

So much of the van conversation could be esoteric, about furthering the playing and what we strived to find in the moment-to-moment connection onstage. We searched for words to describe language that has no words, only feeling and sound. We dismantled the emotional nuance of set lists.

How strange and beautiful our outlook, an innocence. There was an elaborate plan around sleeping in truck stops:

we would traipse through the first stop at 4:00 a.m., brush our teeth, clean up, change for sleep, then drive down the road to the next stop and park without getting out so no one knew we were pajamaed inside. The bass player's cot lay across the front seats, the guitarist was on the bench, and I slept on a pad on top of the bass cabinet.

I woke one morning on a big metal planet, rolling and rumbling as it turned. I opened my eyes to a beautiful white design of still snowflakes in a metal sky and fell in love with the vision until I saw it for what it was, frost on the van ceiling and semi-trucks ringing us, pumping diesel fumes into my dreams.

As we drove from one venue to the next, a different city and a different rock club every day for a year, our conversations could be of farm animals and motor homes and fireflies in the corn fields. The dialogue trailed for miles, then the rolling, constant drives would be solitary, headphones and naps and writing and dreaming.

One additional person changed the dynamic. Three was the only way to keep the tenuous relationship working. There were cracks for sure, and later, as one person crumbled, so the whole thing. But back then, how joined at the hip we were.

There was no one lifting or selling us. We had a booking agent at the end of a phone line, that was it. We decided in an instant to leave, three minds combining in a flash of New Jersey sunset. Leave our partners and apartments and city and jobs to live together indefinitely in a silver Econoline van, all so we could play our instruments, so we could be onstage every night. That moment of decision to leave fused us. We all chose the same thing, and it chose us.

No one could know how much bullshit we had to listen to, or how quickly we could see through the promises of old men. All the phony record deals and insinuations of stardom. All the subtle slights from other musicians, all the soundmen and promoters and bartenders and their dismissive, insulting ways.

We got good at the game. We learned how to smile and take it, take the advice or condescending remarks, and out of that create a monster of sound. Just smile and take it, and then when it's our turn we'll tear off heads with volume and aggression, slam that kick drum through hearts and nail that snare drum to the back of skulls. They are going to be kissing our ass at the end of the set.

How deep our forgiveness, because they just don't know. Rock and roll is a boys' club. We were never hot enough or scary enough or wry enough or in on the joke enough or relaxed enough or just plain enough to be in the club. How strange and special our own club was.

We were never on the inside, so we created a concrete triad of our own. Even now that we haven't spoken in twenty years, the bond is still there. There are no three people in the world who know this story but us, who know this passion and anger and love as we lived it.

We figured we would work harder, that maybe work was the way in. We took it all on, three of us, driving and loading and selling and playing. Every day another city.

For six weeks we drove overnight, loaded into the Warped Tour festival at 11:00 a.m., and slept in Texas summer heat on the concrete shade near the toilets. I played drums so hot my calf had burns on it from the floor tom legs. We carried equipment through twenty thousand people, over grass and trash and through rainstorms, drove four more hours, loaded the gear into another venue as the band before us finished their set, left every remaining ounce of sweat onstage, loaded back into the van, then drove all night to do it again.

I did the driving for that tour, and I will always marvel at my stamina as if it were someone else's. I don't know how I did that. All the other bands on the tour in buses, with the after-show barbecues—well, we were never a part of that. We weren't in the club.

We finally missed one show, because when I started hallucinating highway frogs racing the van, I pulled over to sleep for an hour. We woke five hours later, sitting straight up, drooling in our seats while the world of the gas station went on around us.

I don't know anyone who could drive like that, and I don't know anyone who would be asked. I did it for the sake of getting onstage every night, which was all I wanted, profoundly.

I loved this music. I loved this band. I loved this instrument, and I still do. This is what I can't explain, that it was all because playing drums opened a channel to the divine for sometimes just forty-five minutes a night.

The joy of it. Being carried away by the music and watching it move my limbs in this ability for rhythm is a glory unto God. The wild nights were a prize that came with the appreciation. Drums beat open the party, with the antics and the liquor and drugs and the gorgeous combining of bodies that happened in the dark hours after the show.

I get to live in joy when I am onstage. I imagine others find this elsewhere, having children or through work, but this is mine, and I want to feel this every night. I want to prolong it with people who share it and feel it too.

How sweet and in love I was with all of them, one in every town, yet I truly cared and loved them, if only for just one night. How powerful it felt to hold the cards because of talent and joy onstage, to finally be the chooser. I would see myself in the mirror of the club and when my bandmembers stood beside me, I would become more beautiful because we were together, the light of three shining wildness, grace, sexual and creative power. I would take that with me through the night, into the venue, onto the stage, and after.

This kind of morality, gorgeous nights of music and love, can be detracted forever, but what vast pleasure we shared. We lay on lawns talking about the construction of the universe and every dream in it. We watched the moon rise over a field of bison in a pickup truck that sailed in stars. We fell together in the middle of a sweaty discotheque that signaled the end of rock music and in that moment, we stopped caring.

This was our version of a girls' club. Carrying an eight-by-ten bass cabinet down steep, concrete stairs, into a basement studio, we watched as stiletto heels swayed into the dance party. How funny it was, sweating and straining and watching those gorgeous clothes and bodies pass by. The guitarist said, "How stupid we must be. *This* is what we decided to do to get laid . . ." We almost dropped the cabinet down the stairs in convulsive laughter.

There was no other choice for us. We were never a part of that club either, and trying to be like those women never worked. We were built to carry gear.

No epic story of a journey of women could we cling to. There is no female Odysseus. We forged our own saga, and somewhere in our limited little story a new archetype was being written. We weren't warriors, we weren't princesses, we weren't damaged or raging or crazy or searching for shelter. But we were born for this.

It was so precious because it was never easy, and we thrived on difficulty. We were smart and strong and kind and funny and never fit in. So when we found our instruments, we said yes. Yes to driving, yes to loading, yes to playing, yes to getting dressed in truck stops or on strangers' front lawns, yes to living on five dollars a day and to being so close with two other people all day and all night. No number of miles was too much, no show too far, no schedule too rigorous. This is what it's like to have three people agree to it all, no matter how hard and how high. The body gets beat and bloody and we keep moving forward, through injury and illness and insult and argument. We wear pain like a badge of honor.

We fought once in the redwood forest of California, an excruciating argument that widened all the cracks that would eventually end the band. We fought right up until the time we had to get in the van and drive 2,000 miles to Minneapolis, and not a word was said for the whole drive. We didn't stop to sleep, just silently rotated drivers. We paused at gas stations and ate at a Chinese restaurant in Montana. We were the only three people in the restaurant, sitting at different tables in the dining room.

When we arrived at the venue, we took the stage in front of more people than we had ever played for, and in the middle of the first song the guitar stopped working. It took her five minutes of scrambling around like a rat to get it running. For five minutes the bass and I kept playing, as was our protocol, kept playing the same part over and over and over waiting for the guitar to jump back in, which eventually it did in a roaring, climactic moment.

In those five minutes, all the anger dissipated. My heart went out to her, watching the onstage panic. We fused again. At the end of the show we were speaking, same as always.

Words were of so little use in the communication. Maybe we would have lasted longer if we had found words instead of intuition and waveforms.

Some of the promoters and musicians and soundmen understood our journey. There is a network of brother bands I still to this day love like family. They made it easy to keep going. They respected the three, loved the power, recognized this was not their saga, but wanted to see us succeed. The respect meant so much. They saw the struggle we had before us. They saw the value of it.

People brought us to their homes and set us up to sleep and made us food and invited us into their lives and made the journey a magic ride into the heart of humanity. There was rarely an ulterior motive other than love of music. Because I played my drums, I got to taste such spirit and generosity. I have known firsthand the openness of the American heart and the beauty of people who love heavy rock and roll. People rooted for this new female story. How strange and wonderful humanity can be, how music unites us.

Only now when I look back, I see so clearly the band never had a chance for anything more than what we got. We worked like an explosion instead of a slow burn. That was the only way we knew. The cracks deepened when we stopped traveling so much, when all the issues we never dealt with personally or together got wider and harder. One day we were broken, with no way of repairing it.

In Iowa, we cancelled a show. We drove up to the venue and were just too tired. We cancelled the show. That was when I knew the band would end. When we stopped accepting what we had been dealt, there was no place for us.

The end of a band is like no other drama. The incriminations and psychological torture and black heartache came from realizing we were never going to be more. We were shortsighted to never plan for more. The fiery explosion of such an ending reverberates like the last crash cymbal of the last note, then is lost to time.

Sometimes, while I was driving, the yellow line would lend itself to fantasy. I would think about what I would say on the podium if I won a Grammy. In my vision, it was always the three standing there, the power of three shining on the screen, for the first time winning. It would be the same thing I might say now: *Somewhere across the country, a group of musicians are carrying their equipment up metal stairs to the back door of a club, past the dumpsters and out of a beat-up Econoline van. They're grabbing a beer, setting up the gear, asking around for a place to stay after the show, laying out their CDs and T-shirts in hope of gas money. They're rocking it, and they have no idea the Grammys are happening. They are in love with the journey. I'm in love with the journey.*

I'm in love with the journey. I'm in love with playing my drums, with playing in a band, with musicians and touring and all of it. What happens in the van is sacred. What happens onstage is sacred. What happens over years of playing an instrument, that progress is sacred.

People ask, Are you still playing? If you had a taste of it, you could never give it up.

12   I fly into Denver the night before the rest of the band to acclimate to the mile-high altitude. Playing drums is such physical exertion, and the lack of oxygen in the mountains affects me in ways I dread.

First, I can't lift my arms very high when I play or I feel unbearably weak, as if all the blood has drained onto the drum riser. I change my motions, keeping my arms closer to my sides, with smaller movements. Making this adjustment pulls me into the trap of my thoughts as I play.

At altitude, sometimes in the middle of a song my brain shuts off and not in the way that makes for great drumming. I do silly things on the drums that sound as though I have slid off the drum stool. I will be in the flow, sunk into the song, and something in my being says, *Wait a minute, what am I doing here? I know how to play drums?* Everything crumbles.

All this onstage struggle exists purely because I have an excuse for it. The problem of altitude is a kite string my brain uses to keep a hold on me, preventing me from floating into the clear sky of no-thought. Here is potential difficulty to latch on to, so my brain does what it is built for: setting off alarms, keeping me wary and threatened.

I watch as my thoughts keep trying to snap me back into this "reality" with the threat of danger. I am floating along just fine, then comes the thought, *We are at altitude! Stay focused so you don't do something dumb!* I proceed then to launch into a drum fill that sounds as if I am being slowly run over by a truck.

I do get better at all this, though, as time goes on.

I remember to breathe, to relax the center of my body as I play. Anticipation of difficulty manifests problems, so it's important to stay relaxed. I use my breath to locate the stillness at the heart of the song, resisting the intrusion of nagging and anticipating thoughts.

Worry rises and dissipates like clouds when I don't react.

I was driving to pick up some rental gear. My eyes started to blur and cross with the pain of headache, and I had to pull off the road for safety.

The Denver airport lies in the middle of a golden, empty basin of vast fields, so the only place I could find to stop was a half-built housing development. I pulled into a cul-de-sac of vacant homes and lay in a ball on the front seat for ninety minutes, until I could focus my eyes enough to drive to the airport to meet the band and lay my hands on the magic migraine medicine I know Gretchen carries with her.

As I was lying there, in the front seat of a rental vehicle on a random, just-built road, sounds of construction around me and prairie wind gently shaking the car, I felt pretty balanced. My head was a misery, sure, and I lay curled in a ball with my hands pressed against my eyes so no light could get in. Yet, when I woke from dozing and caught a brief glance of sky, I saw a color of blue that doesn't happen at sea level. Clouds whiter than cotton blew by, and in the split second my eyes opened, the shapes imprinted themselves on the other side of the pain. I watched them roll across the dark side of my eyelids.

It was a marvel to be so randomly disconnected from my regular path. Because of the pain and my tendency toward drama, I had some thoughts about death. How strange it would be for someone to find this body here, on a side street in a random neighborhood thirteen hundred miles from home, curled up in a minivan with drum paraphernalia and forty band T-shirts under the hatchback. My mind moved through the path the investigators would take trying to figure out who I was and how I had died and the ensuing mystery, remembered for the question: What was she doing there?

I am keenly aware of the observer within my awareness through this whole experience. I watch as I pull off the highway and focus all attention on finding a place to stop driving before I *have* to stop driving. I watch as I lie there, a tiny speck on beige upholstery, on a small planet in a vast universe, suffering and yet safe. I am peaceful in the knowledge that this too will pass. I have felt worse. I have been sicker. I will live another day, and in that day there may be no migraine, no matter what my brain is forecasting now.

Who am I? Who is it that watches as I go through this? It is the same one watching as we go through accidents and emotional stress and shock. Awareness watches as the moments change. They always change. Right now, I am alive. The body is in pain. Now, let's see what the next moment will be like.

I watch poor, sick, uncomfortable Clem, who struggles. Here is the vibrating consciousness manifesting existence. Here, that still and joyous center.

This must be what my first meditation teacher, the dear S. N. Goenka, called "the art of living." It is not about arranging life so nothing will go wrong, since we are on a train with vastly unpredictable stops and starts. The art of living depends on us resting in awareness, fully present as the trip plays out.

13 After the show I let it all go: the frustrations, the drive, the moments of delight onstage, and the struggle, the fatigue, the regret of habits. In the physical exhaustion, all of it dropped away. The veils of reality thinned. I started to gaze at the people around me, dancing or laughing or walking by or checking IDs or carrying drinks. I started to imagine I could see each one as their true self.

A person's outer aspect, their demeanor, their aura, even sometimes their behavior, is like a little window. As I looked, I started to see each person's essence in a flash.

The tough guy at the door had a delicate, joyful, child-like energy that shimmered. The waitress was a shower of soft sparks emanating peace. The pierced, undulating dancer was an ancient glow. The out of place–looking guy watching the dancing was a permeating power, like a lion.

My friend came dancing up and was a silver spiral of electricity. There was so much delight, so much love, all around me.

I remembered words my mentor sent me from her teacher:

> *Humans must learn they can instantly change their energy patterns into patterns of beauty. Humans cling to angles, where really roundness would be more fulfilling and aligned with true nature. Even round furniture, gardens and architecture would help*

people awaken. It is circular, the flower flow-
ing forth from its center, and light turning back
onto light. Awakening is simplicity.[2]

I remembered to breathe in a circle. I became lighter as I merged with all these beings. I imagined showers of sparks raining into the room and infusing everyone with delight. My heart broke open as the band played and the audience danced.

Is this a bias, to think each person I see is holy, awakened, infinite?

14

The streets were joy. My heart was joy. My days were spent reading and writing and being with the pug and meditating. I was happy when I woke and then all day and night. I read the words of spiritual teachers and of history and of the beautiful flow of my culture awakening to a collective heart, rising through the rocky passages from deep cellars of wrong ways.

Once I started driving, this state of mind lasted a few hours, then began to make room for another way of being apparently more appropriate for a weekend of shows.

Rock bands and their stories are a narrative part of my identity. The wildness and outlaw living a myth and a pattern. A trigger. I am a rock drummer, and as I drive, I drop the experience of introspection from my days off and connect with a field of information that steers toward excess.

Maybe I jump into the mind because I have to pay attention. Directions and traffic and equipment and hotels and meals and misunderstandings. Set times. New songs. Tickets sold. I force myself to focus, or I cause problems.

I see how when I am in my head I give in to impulses with abandon. It's as if when I follow my thoughts, nothing is thoughtful. Everything in me grasps, choices are made out of compulsion. I have so little impulse control. My corporeal body clings to old patterns, and need drives me to satiate chemical patterns of pleasure. I drink Red Bull and whiskey. I curse at drivers. I eat too much and eat ridiculous food: Rice Krispies Treats and questionable roadside burritos.

Not only is this Clem addicted to the sensations of poor judgment and need, but there is also a deep pleasure in the regret of these actions and the ensuing vow to do differently. I fail. I judge myself harshly. Then, beautiful days of abstinence and clarity, the mind a small radio signal in an ocean of silent flow. Misery is captured and released, captured and released, like butterflies caught in the story of my life, over and over.

In the little park, the pug sniffed around. I sat myself down in the morning sun.

I'd hit the right hour for dragonflies, because there were a number of them zipping around the park, so beautiful and careeningly free. I recalled Thoreau and his thoughts about the innocence of nature.[3]

I remembered that dragonflies have sex midflight and flashed on the word "ecstatic." I remembered a boy I loved for a night while on tour in Asheville, North Carolina, after a walk through an ancient cemetery on an autumn afternoon, leaves and dragonflies chasing sunlight falling.

Suddenly, I saw a dragonfly disappear, like a pop, out of the air. One minute barreling through the sky, one minute gone. It was funny—it didn't seem out of the ordinary that this being, flying, would vanish in front of my eyes. Dragonflies are so chaotic and authoritative that surprise wasn't my first response.

I thought of that giant particle accelerator in Switzerland and how scientists discovered particles that would disappear, then mysteriously show up somewhere else. Or how one particle can be in two places at once.[4]

I spent a little time sitting there, thinking about that dragonfly and how it blipped out. I imagined a small pocket of molecules arranged in space and time in a brand-new way. As he flitted across the park, he found that little wormhole and in an instant was transported to a whole different part of the park entirely, or a different year even.

I was thinking that maybe this sort of thing happens all the time, but because we have a fixed idea of reality, we never notice. Like the story of the indigenous Australians, how when they saw the explorers' ships, it took them several days to even recognize that anything was there on the horizon. Those ships didn't exist in their reality, so they didn't see them.[5]

I look around thinking, *What is here that I am not seeing because I don't expect to see it?* I imagine alien spaceships hanging in the sky above me. I imagine the deceased walking among us. I imagine wormhole portals that would be so easy to use, if I could only see. Maybe things are coming and going, popping in and out, all the time.

I arrived to the rehearsal studio and put on an AC/DC song for a change. There are a couple of songs I was never able to play well when I was playing in an AC/DC band, and now and then I revisit them to see if I can make any headway.

The songs I could never manage are the very up-tempo ones: "Whole Lotta Rosie," "Let There Be Rock." The secret of AC/DC's drummer, Phil Rudd, is that playing AC/DC is a lesson in how to swing. Drummers are always talking about how basic those beats are, but *you* try playing a simple beat of four on the floor and making a stadium full of people lose their minds. It's all about how that hi-hat swings. The way Rudd plays it, he could move anyone to dance.

At those fast tempos, I psych myself out. My wrist gets tired quickly. I start clutching the stick in a clawed fist, and all the feel in the groove goes away. I sound like I don't know how to play drums.

I turned on "Let There Be Rock" and immediately had that familiar, defeated feeling. I wanted to give up. I sat for a minute, and the dragonfly came to mind. I guess he found that wormhole again, for now here he was in my head.

What about this reality am I not seeing?

Here I am, with this feeling of dread, knowing that my wrist is going to tense, that I will give up midway through. I anticipate the familiar feeling of shame and defeat.

I thought, what if the thing I'm not seeing is that the song is actually possible? If I believed the song were easy, my body would relax completely. I would feel joy in the movement. What if I *play the fucking song* and stop stressing out about it?

I restarted the track. It's a long song for another thing, which makes it such a beast. It is difficult to play something so fast for so long.

Never mind!

It doesn't matter how long the song is. If it is easy and joyful, I can play forever.

I took a deep breath and started that hi-hat swing. I made sure to keep breathing deeply and evenly. I witnessed my hand and my wrist. The blood was warm in my veins and the tendons loose and limber.

Every time a thought rose about difficulty, I had a twinge of stress, sometimes in my forearm, sometimes in my wrist, sometimes in my shoulder, sometimes in my back, sometimes in my stomach. I relaxed that area and breathed into it. I breathed. I relaxed. I kept thinking, *I love to play this song.*

About halfway through, I noticed I was feeling some joy but tried not to get wrapped up in that either. I didn't want to jinx it. It occurred to me it might be better to notice when I felt peaceful. Just feel really peaceful while I play this song I love, that I love to play.

I managed it all the way, kept the swing up, and ended the song in joy, as if I could keep going forever.

All done! I'm going home, mission accomplished.

Not really. I congratulated myself for a bit, then started banging out some other stuff that drives me nuts. Let there be rock indeed! Thank you, little dragonfly. I hope you're in some alternate reality, having sex right now.

How to play a Led Zeppelin song in twelve steps.

Step One. Love Led Zeppelin. I wonder sometimes about what makes a drummer a household name. There certainly aren't many who are. Name recognition goes to the singer, sometimes the guitarist. It is pretty rare for the nonmusician to connect with the person at the back of the stage. Unless they at some point sing a song (Ringo and Dave Grohl and Levon Helm), or construct elaborate showmanship vessels (Tommy Lee), often the drummer's name is lost. How did John Bonham become one of those who are celebrated as much as any of the other guys in the band?

I chalk it up to feel. I chalk it up to love. There is an underlying emotion to the music that comes from the bottom up, rises through the songs like a rich and vital thing, infusing the whole ensemble with a powerful, settled feel and intangible poignancy. Any musician can learn how to play any Led Zeppelin song of course, but to make it feel anything like the original, you must start with a love for that visceral, emotive foundation.

Step Two. You had better love it, because you can't listen to the song enough. Bonham played with a confidence and swagger that leaves no room for unsteadiness or question of form. You should feel the changes in your veins. Rising above math while playing is the goal. Listen as you're falling asleep, and let the dark and perfectly recorded sound carry you into dreams. Know the voice of each instrument, not just the drums.

It helps if you spent time at a very young age absorbing the material, sitting in rooms with your friends marveling at the atmosphere and power. It helps if you spent nights with your hand on your clock radio, feeling completely alone in the middle of your family, your school, your teenage life, and this music unraveled out of the small speaker, wrapping you in hope for a future wide with beauty.

Step Three. Chart it out. Name the parts: intro, verse, pre-chorus, chorus, C-part. Any significant change in the song merits a new name. Count them out. Remember that Zeppelin loves to make it interesting. Sections change after seven measures rather than predictable eights, or they will add a measure of two-four time at the end of a series to trip you up. Create your own hieroglyphics for this purpose. I have a friend who writes as if she were Mozart, penning the score in perfect, small writing. I have another friend who developed an elaborate language of symbols that look like graffiti tags.

Drum notation is very easy to read and use, and still I create my own little world on the page. Sometimes I chart it and then never use the chart. Just the practice of writing it out embeds the form more deeply in the subconscious.

Step Four. Learn the basic grooves of each part by playing them over and over with no regard to the slight changes within the parts. The song needs to feel good, and it will feel good when you own the groove. Notice the movement of the body and the conversation between your limbs. When I play "The Ocean," I feel the accents on the snare working with the rise and fall of the hi-hat and bass patterns to move my body like a steam piston sliding across a floor. I get to be a machine there, all swing and torsion as I dance with space and time, slam the snare hand down and bring the foot to the one.

Step Five. Now tie the parts together. When you come to transitions and drum fills that are troublesome, the real buckling down begins. Develop a system for writing out the fills. Get some good headphones and a looping program. Sticking is everything. The left hand starts this fill, or maybe it's the foot. More than likely, Bonham is starting the drum fill in the middle of the phrase before you think it should start. Try to play the fill on the snare drum only, then between the snare and the foot, then try to move around the drums.

Play it one million times until the musicality of the fill becomes its own beast. Then, practice landing exactly right into the next part. Landing on that first note coming out of the fill is the most important place in the song. You can flub a fill onstage, and everyone will think you're just being creative as long as that first hit out of the fill is in time. Loop a bar of the groove, then the fill, then a bar of the groove on the other side. Make the transitions seamless.

Step Six. Spend some time lamenting your technique. Regret all the things that kept you from practicing, beat yourself up about your lazy tendencies, the years when you didn't play drums at all. Then, straighten up, buckle down, work on your technique.

When your chops are a deterrent to being able to play a particularly tricky part, here comes the woodshedding. You won't be able to play a Bonham song without a certain amount of technique. Improve your technique. Sit in a practice room and do mindless patterns over and over until your muscles begin to remember. Sometimes, in order to get the thing working for a live show, you will have to find a simpler way to play the part while you keep practicing, sometimes for years, to master that particular technique. Meanwhile, simplify the part so it has a relative sound and feel and transitions the song in the same way. This is Bonham, so if you're like me, some of these techniques are lifetime goals. Be humble, accept the limitation for the time being, repeat this step endlessly.

Step Seven. Now you get to play through the song. Play until you stumble, loop the problem area until it's resolved, then start the song from the beginning and try it again. Remember that a slow speed is your great friend in learning. Patience is your ally. Extend kindness to yourself as much as to anyone you love. Playing something wrong at tempo over and over will just reinforce the wrong. Slow the part down until you can play it correctly, then watch your speed improve with repetition.

Step Eight. Try to play without the soundtrack. When you sit down with the band, you are going to realize you're being cued by things on the album that you're not hearing in the practice studio. Often, it's an extra guitar track that has been given up in the impossibility of playing three guitar lines on one guitar. Sometimes, it's an effect Jimmy Page added in the magic of the studio. The closest you can get to playing the whole song with just a click track, not listening to the song in your ears while you play, the more your band will be impressed when it comes time to play together and the better you will be at establishing the foundation rather than following down the tracks of a train wreck.

Step Nine. As for feel, remember to lean back. Lean way back. John Bonham took his time. He took his time until he felt it was interesting to speed it up a little, make a little racket. But underneath it all, most Bonham songs live behind the beat. The push and pull of time beneath tempo is the glorious part of drumming. You get to affect the way the song feels while placing yourself behind or in front of the metronome click, or right on it. This isn't about how fast the song is. This is about feel. Bonham feels like he has something to say, and you're going to wait for it, and when it reaches you, it is exactly what you wanted to hear. This is an education in authority and charisma.

Step Ten. If you can, watch a video of Bonham playing the song live. It's rare I can tell exactly what he's doing, but sometimes, I get a little light bulb. Oh, he's hitting that crash cymbal with the left hand, not the right. Oh, he's leaning into that section of the song. I see his body tense and release into the fill. I watch him play that live version of "Immigrant Song" on the collection *How The West Was Won*, and he comes flying at those drums like a storm breaking loose from the ether. Imitate the attitude of the drummer, and sometimes the attitude reflects in your playing.

Step Eleven. Learn some background. Bonham loved Gene Krupa, so I listen to Gene Krupa to uncover something of his sensibility: those big ringy drums, that settled yet pyrotechnic way of playing, that joy. I know from reading biographies that Bonham and Robert Plant had a special personal connection. I listen to the way the vocals and drums speak with each other, the way the drums give the vocal space.

Step Twelve. Finally, it's time to make it your own. Drums are such an athletic event that to play someone's parts can be like getting into their body. You have dreams where you're walking arm in arm with him, and you know how it feels to hug him. You hear what he heard, and you start to understand the reason he wrote the pattern: the little hiccup in the guitar riff that signals the odd snare hit, the sway of the bass line that influences the hi-hat swing. You start getting an idea of where he might go should something out of the ordinary happen— say, should the singer come in late to the verse. You start to understand why you feel a slight rush in a part on the record, how it makes sense to slow it back down in this place here. You start to expand into improvisation and realize that one of your favorite things about Bonham's playing is a feeling of exuberant exploration, an ability to push the limit while always making it feel so good.

Then, one day, the horizon shifts, and you fully hear the song, all the elements beyond your dissection and mathematics and practice, and you play the song the way you remember hearing it that first time, with the light dim in your little room, the dream of the future coming out of your clock radio as you close your eyes and hear a universe of magic in the sound of a bass drum.[6]

John Bonham was a powerful drummer, no question. He was powerful in all the ways our culture references power: heavy-hitting, with an ability to let loose a thunder, relentless and pounding.

All true, but I would argue that Bonham's real power, and the reason he is beloved by so many, is in the subtleness of his groove. The reason Zeppelin songs feel the way they do, that exquisite "something" that has been chased by rock bands for half a century, is the translation on drums of the delicacy of power.

Bonham's groove is not just behind the beat, creating a settled feeling. His rhythm sits in a magic sliver of timekeeping that somehow slips into the center of our knowing. He waits, he dances, he finds the longing in our hearts for a dream of perfection that translates as love.

A great example of this is "Fool in the Rain." You hear the keyboard on top, its boxy rhythm announcing itself, and underneath, the drums slide the melody into our soul. This is the power of subtlety, the power of understanding, the power of emotion. It is unmistakable, elusive, so easy to dismiss.

I see many drummers play Bonham's parts, and many, including myself, exaggerate heavy-handedness in the pursuit of the power of his playing. The best of them know to get close to the implicit communication in the feel, the subtlety and heart.

I wonder if what we hear in Bonham's playing is pure confidence, pure knowing without question. In this we might separate Bonham the person from Bonham the player. He seemed to struggle in his life, but behind the drum kit he seemed to never question what he was saying.

Maybe this knowing is what we pick up on when we listen to Bonham play. We tune into a field of truth that rises in our own life, if only in glimpses—the power of truth and knowing.

There are many parallels between my father and John Bonham. Bonham was six years younger, but both were prideful of their working-class status and the work ethic that confers. They were built the same, with broad chests and heavy limbs, yet agile. They both were deeply emotional men, yet their ability to express that emotion was stymied by the culture and its rigid framework of what a man was to be.

I am quite compassionate to the men of this era and their inability to express pain. My father's escape was music, and food. John Bonham's escape was music, and alcohol. They were both volatile and could behave badly in fits of rage through which that power expressed itself externally.

We learn when looking back to forgive the men, not the behavior. The way I do this is by becoming deeply aware of the love that was longing to be expressed, the softness, the delicacy of feeling that ran like a torrent through each of them. With my father, I felt that unexpressed emotion in a million little ways. I wish he had found more ways to let me, or anyone, into his suffering. With John Bonham, I hear it in his drumming, in every fragile and poignant clue that speaks his melody.

18 "Good Times Bad Times." The first song on the first Led Zeppelin album. John Bonham might not have had any say about what song came first on this record, so assume that in each track here he is showing the best of himself. Each song is a proclamation, the statement he has chosen to make to the world about who he is and what he can do. Maybe in each song he was thinking of all the ways he could show us what was important to him in drumming, setting us up to know we will always be safe in his hands.

It is indeed all here in this song. We talk about how silence is another voice in great music, and we get the lesson right out of the gate. The declaration. The authority. For silence gives authority, since the drummer and the band and that first beat lie naked in our perception of power. If the band rushes the entry, the audience searches for feel. If they drag it, too bluesy. But the drums straddle both power and blues. This is Zeppelin, power and blues.

Making the song feel good has so much to do with the kick drum. It is the pulse in the dance song, the relentless pounding on the quarter note that shakes the booty. In rock songs, it is often that same pulse, called "four on the floor," which means you're pounding all four quarter notes in a measure with the right foot on the biggest drum. AC/DC are masters of this.

In rock, the kick drum, also called the bass drum, is where the time is kept. In jazz, the time is announced on the big ride cymbal the drummer plays with, for right-handed drummers, the right hand. But in rock, the pulse comes from the ground up, and the drummer's relationship with the kick drum says so much about the kind of drummer they are. Some stomp it, some accent it delicately, some play it like an assault.

John Bonham was known for having, as Jimi Hendrix said, "a right foot like a rabbit." This means his foot was a lot busier than four on the floor. He was adding accents and flourishes that created a rumble, syncopated interest, and the thunder when they speak of his "thunder of drums." He was able to roll on the bass drum with small and powerful movements involving his ankle, an intuitive relationship with the way the foot flurries on the pedal and, therefore, the drum.

There are wide debates about how he did this and lessons on how to get your own foot up to speed. At the end of the day though, the magic of John Bonham's foot is not so much about the quickness but about where he places the beats and therefore affects the feel of the song. Zeppelin songs feel like no others. There is a reason the drum beat from "When the Levee Breaks" is the second most sampled song on the planet by DJs and hip-hop artists. It feels that good.

The kick pattern in "Good Times Bad Times" escapes me. I get closer, then farther away, a rubber band of ability that is maddening. It seems every drummer in the world has this ability to play the pattern but me. This is a strange thing, because I have put in the years.

This inability causes me quite a bit of grief. I go along, happily confident in how I play, and, especially when the band gets quite busy, I feel myself embodying an energy that feels very present. I think I have a realistic image of where I sit in the pantheon of drummers, humble always at my narrow technique. It may be narrow, but I do it pretty well.

This elusive foot pattern makes me question my drumming overall. Have I just been fooling myself all along?

I have spent some time, not only in the endless physical exercises required, but in the energetic realm, examining that which resists this movement. I work to develop a relaxation that comes from the center of my ankle. I am trying to remove self-consciousness from my foot. Can I tie the rhythm of that kick drum pedal to the melody Bonham plays for the patterns to flow effortlessly? This is the work.

I think about relaxation a lot through my days. When my internal space, my inner atrium of awareness, becomes chaotic, I imagine the color green, breathe into the stillness of emerald, relax into it. My mind does occasionally race, but I welcome the racing when I will it. When writing or having a conversation, I want that free flow of intellect. Most other times, I want to feel myself in spaciousness, allowing impressions to rise and be felt and then go. I am an experiencer; that's my job now. I think it may be everybody's job now.

Relaxation and presence. I search for a way to be fully present in my physical body. I fought being in my body for most of my life. It started naturally, as I was always much more interested in reading and studying than I was in sports. I started to see myself as someone who preferred the intellect over the physical.

Then, the dieting and the self-flagellation that came for me early, a cultural loop of negativity that begins young and doesn't seem to have an age limit. Too fat, too thin, wrong body shape, too young, too old, not pretty enough, on and on. The development of active hatred and attack of the physical form.

Then, the spiritual openings and the ability to leap into the true self, forsake the personality, and find beautiful places of dissociation, of escape from this manifestation of form.

Even when drumming, I am searching for that place in which the physical happens in the background, on its own, while the mind is overtaken by energy and waveform.

Drumming is also the way to come back to physicality. I realize this more over time. The blazing delight of the body while drumming brings me right here, present in deep appreciation. The mind may fall into that detached center of awareness, but the body moves in a glorious circle around that awareness, spiraling in to the Now. It is a spectacular feeling, to recognize the strength of the back, the fluidity of shoulders and hips, the pivot point in the core on which everything turns. There is no necessity for me to be anywhere or anything else.

So when the foot is resisting the pattern in this song, I give it a break. I am learning to speak kindly to my body, when for so long only harsh words have been spoken. One day, I will forget that this struggle with this song was an issue, and the pattern will just begin happening. I will laugh that it took me so long to accomplish something so simple. Or, I may just never be able to do it. Either way, I am still a drummer, still a human in a human body, flawed and perfect at the same time.

19 Nothing was working as I thought it was going to. Everything was hard. I moved to New York to be a writer, to throw my hat in with Capote and Fitzgerald, to rush the steps of Grand Central as Salinger had, to breathe the early morning fog in Washington Square where Cather had walked. To ride the ferry, very merry, and to stand at cocktail parties where editors and writers traded bon mots.

It was 1992. I stood behind the bar at a diner, Tom Waits on the stereo and an array of working stiffs asking for stiff drinks. The glamour of uptown literary society never passed Broadway and Bleecker. There was a stratosphere above Fourteenth Street where such things existed, but it might as well have been across an ocean, across a galaxy of time.

I spent many weekends of my childhood in the thrall of old movies. When I thought of literary society, I could almost hear the clink of Rosalind Russell's martini glass as she stood in a many-roomed apartment on the Upper East Side, with editors from *The New Yorker* and Knopf, fast-talking current events with quick-witted men in slightly crumpled suits. Even today I can conjure that daydream, and now I can taste the martini. I had no business thinking I was going to magically find myself there. I had no idea how to get within proximity.

Then, standing at the bar at three in the morning, I read Rilke's "For the sake of a single poem":

*Ah, poems amount to so little when you write
them too early in your life. You ought to wait*

and gather sense and sweetness for a whole lifetime, and a long one if possible, and then, at the very end, you might perhaps be able to write ten good lines. For poems are not, as people think, simply emotions (one has emotions early enough)—they are experiences. For the sake of a single poem, you must see many cities, many people and Things . . . Only when they have changed into our very blood, into glance and gesture, and are nameless, no longer to be distinguished from ourselves—only then can it happen that in some very rare hour the first word of a poem arises in their midst and goes forth from them.[7]

That clinched it. I had known nothing. It was a crisis of youth, although to many people twenty-seven years old does not seem so young. It was apparent I had nothing to say. I had a low self-worth, a desire for adventure, and a strong feeling I had never found my place or my people. I wanted to write, but it was baldly obvious I had not lived.

Some of my friends were actively seeking heroin addictions. While this had its glamour, I was born with the ability to wake in anticipatory joy of the coming day. It is a genetic thing, which you would understand should you spend fifteen minutes with my family. I was lucky to be driven to seek my happiness in other ways.

When I was standing at the bar reading Rilke and listening to "Rain Dogs" on the stereo, I said to myself, *I'm tired of being a bartender. I need to see the world to be the writer I dream of being.*

Musicians were in the circle around me. I thought, *I never thought of being a musician before. How about I do that for a living? That way, I could work while traveling.*

It seemed perfectly feasible and no big deal I didn't play an instrument.

I started learning to play drums.

This is a favorite story from my time with Fred Klatz, the drum teacher who turned out to be the best drum teacher in New York City, someone whom I love dearly to this day.

I was attempting an exercise in which I was playing four different patterns with each of my limbs, and he was asking me to count a different pattern out loud. If I thought too hard about any one piece, say my left foot, the whole thing would fall apart. It kept falling apart.

He said, "You know where your mind has to be for this? You know when you're looking all over the house for your glove, and after five minutes of searching you look down and realize you've been holding it the whole time? Put your mind there."

Instantly, I could do it. One metaphor, and the world changed.

20

Her first job in New York was in a restaurant on MacDougal Street in the West Village. It had been a diner in the center of the 1960s, and the proprietor had been an owner of Cafe Wha?, where many of her musical heroes started. Now, it was a Mexican restaurant that drew bridge and tunnel in, with its tattered awning claiming hundreds of tequilas.

It really was her first job, the first job that was necessary to keep her housed and fed. She took it seriously and worked very hard.

She waitressed with a girl who rented a room in her apartment on Twelfth Street, between Avenues A and B, and they became roommates. Lisa was a fiery Italian and showed the girl the ropes. Lisa was a dancer and a drummer, and drums were set up in the corner of the big room, her room. She played in the afternoons. You could do that in the East Village, make that kind of noise in the afternoons in apartment buildings. The man next door played the same song on the clarinet for the three years the girl lived in that apartment.

Her room was eight feet by eight feet. The window looked onto an airshaft. In the apartment across the five-foot space lived a Puerto Rican family she never met but for whom she developed great fondness. The family came alive at 6:00 a.m. Even though she often worked until 4:00 a.m., she loved hearing their mornings. She couldn't fight the noise, so she imagined they were her family, getting breakfast ready for whenever she decided to wake.

She was hell-bent on decorating her space, the first one truly her own. She put down sticky black-and-white tiles and painted the walls white with teal accents. She bought a twin bed, and when Dylan slept there, his six-foot-five frame wrapped around her, and the bed magically grew.

He worked in the restaurant with her. A waitress in film school asked the two of them to be in her movie. They shot in an abandoned apartment in Brooklyn. Dylan had to kill her, strangling her while the cameras shot into the medicine cabinet mirror.

While the camera crew was arranging props and scenes, the two sat on dingy carpet in an empty room in dying light and fell in love.

Some kind of microbiology connects people like this, and it doesn't happen very often in life. They were together from that night on. There was drama, a boyfriend looking for her, and she just couldn't care. She was on a kind of rocket ship of a physical and emotional journey scheduled all along.

Dylan was articulate and funny, and his body fit hers perfectly. She adored him. She didn't know how to love anyone. She wasn't insecure or frightened by the depth of it, since what drew them together was like a destiny, or a science. She saw her whole life spin out when she was with him.

No one else saw it. His father didn't care for her, his brothers were confused by their relationship, and his friends would tell him, She just doesn't look like the person you would be with. His mother loved her, but she could see it wasn't going to hold. They were so young, living in New York City. This is when she learned about timing, how time dictates a life. Time was not on their side.

Once, they were in a taxi and the driver was barreling down the streets in a harrowing way. As they shakily exited the ride, Dylan put his hand on the driver's shoulder, startling him. "Don't ever drive like that again." The man, at first taken aback by this huge guy touching him, started to laugh.

That was the amazing quality, that Dylan moved through any stress so easily, so competently. She had never known a man like that, having grown up with a man who was a series of explosions, moody and angry and bossy. She had never known anyone who didn't take his own frustrations out on others.

Dylan was joyful. He was a gorgeous man and made fun of his own looks, poking his chest and laughing about the six-pack stomach he did nothing to cultivate. They made love often, and once, out the window, she could see an old woman washing the dishes in her apartment. The girl felt so happy to be offering something so beautiful, should the woman care to look. The girl was young enough to be under the impression that no one had so loved.

When it ended, the pain was exquisite. She felt her center crack open. She cried all the way to California, plane passengers buying her drinks to shut her up. Nature, science, the laws of biology and the magic of cellular memory, all was pointing to this pairing. They were supposed to have children. They were supposed to grow together into who they were to become.

She didn't realize that she was grieving the realization this kind of traditional life was never going to be in the cards for her. The end of this relationship was the confirmation of her choice for the more difficult path.

She had never wanted children, would say so from a very early age. She had based all her decisions to this point on the dream of a life with creative purpose. The love affair had clouded all that. She was rescued by heartbreak.

What are these things that happen in a life and bring us to now? It may be the case that rather than a linear progression, all our moments are stacked on top of each other, even alternate realities. Maybe there is a reality in which Clem became an English professor and Volvo-driving mommy. Regardless, those early days of magic will always reverberate through these.

21 The dog sits in the window and surveys his garden. He barks now and then at the fluttering leaves, flashes of light between the trees. A mourning dove flies by the window, and the dog seems startled to see the wings spreading and fluttering. Blue jays glide toward us. The jays must have a perch in this old building, in the wall or roof, and they start free-falling into the fig tree below. The dog doesn't bark at the birds. He allows them their rituals.

I drop my awareness into my heart and expand beyond the borders of my skin. The body breathes, the air blows out of my pores. The skin is a membrane through which breath travels.

When a thought arises, a tension might drag through the chest or the stomach or the thighs, a clutching sensation denoting dread or fear or shame or any number of unnamed emotional patterns contracting the body. I invite in these feelings. I don't fight. I let myself feel the power of the emotions, the power of the tension caused by thought.

These patterns of stress are so consuming that for my whole life I have imagined there is nothing else, that these feelings are my whole identity. Now, I feel something underneath these emotions, something still and unchanging and expansive. A different force. It stretches out and fills me; emotions ripple like water at the surface. They sink, and I watch as they pass through.

I intuit a trap door beneath me, and I breathe open the door for the tensions to blow out of the body, out of the self, through the door. I shut it.

The air is heavenly here. Outside, a siren streams through the beautiful blue day, a banner of sound that presents itself, stays for a while, then unwinds into the wind. White moths flutter in the broad sails of the fig tree and hang beside the mandarins for contrast.

I don't see the blue jays now. Maybe they're sleeping or hunting elsewhere. The neighbor has hung silver from a bush in the yard, and I hope that doesn't keep the jays away. Typical earthbound humans, with no regard for the magic blue jays bring.

I wonder what the moths are doing out there among the trees. They seem to spend their days dancing on wisps of air currents, drawing outlines of branches and leaves. My life seems mirrored in their movements. Perhaps if my life were sped up to the timeline of a moth's life, I would be just as a-flutter, just as randomly tracing patterns unseen.

The afternoon rests still and peaceful within me, the dog at my feet and my skin kissed with breezes through the old windowsill. I well up with thankfulness for this reality. What a wonderful creation, a spectacular hologram, with so much detail and beauty. The trolley bell dings, and the wooden chimes clatter. My eyes are open, and I can feel the air move through me as I spread beyond the limits of skin and body.

I feel it all letting go: the constant worry of the physical self, worry about achievement, stress about the future. Now, I am here, a human, being. The past is a dream. The future unveils itself moment to moment. Meaning darts away like the tip of the hummingbird, tracing invisible spirals on the breath of the day.

There she is, a twentysomething standing behind the bar at a diner, playing Continental Rummy with Gus the Drunk and looking out into the still, snowy night. The pink light of a neon sign bathes the restaurant in a rosy glow.

For $2.50 on weekday mornings, you get eggs and meat and toast and coffee. That's what year it is, when breakfast cost $2.50 in New York City. The bar is open from eight in the morning until four the next. During the week, if it is absolutely dead, she gets to close two hours early.

On this night, a couple sits at a table for a late-night snack, and sitting at the bar, Gus the Drunk and Jerry. Gus drinks brandy and milk to ease his ulcer. Jerry drinks coffee. He'll switch to vodka down the road, and the girl will discover why the coffee years are the good ones.

I see her grab the beer taps and imagine steering a big ship through the wake of time. I watch her and feel love and frustration and sorrow, and I marvel at the delicate workings of circumstance and fate. I see her riding the current in the river of my history.

She laughs a lot. Tall, thin, with some curviness so she constantly thinks she's fat. Short red hair she cuts with thinning shears to tease the heaviness. Good skin.

In New York, a bartender is known by their following, and her following consists of the kind of people who make a diner like that home base. She prefers people out of time. She relates. The city moves forward and leaves them all behind, in the small pink diner in the middle of everything. They sit back, watch progress unfold around them.

Later, she will work at a wine bar across the street from Barney's department store. It will seem more suited to her, and yet she will find it boring. That clientele doesn't tell stories to waitresses. There, she gets used to being invisible. At the diner, she is the center.

She stands at the bar asking the world for things, and in the manner of pretty girls who work as bartenders, everything comes to her. Later, she'll wish she'd asked for more.

"I'm out!" She lays her cards down matter-of-factly.

"Ah! I don't know what kind of female voodoo this is here, fuggedaboudit." Gus puts his hand up to his eyes and shakes his head. "You come up to the Bronx, they'll never believe it."

He places the stir straw on the bevnap and pushes the amber water glass toward her. She grabs the ice scooper. She tops off the glass with ice, reaches down to the well rack, pours the brandy and then the milk, pulled from the freezer behind. Gus says that when this card game hit the Bronx, poker was out. It drives him crazy that she wins more than he does.

Jerry chuckles and lights another smoke. "She got you again, Gus."

The girl steps to the coffee maker and refills Jerry's cup on her way to clear plates from the table of diners.

"We'll have the check." She sets the plates on the adjoining table, whips the pad from her apron, adds the tax, totals the check, and lays it facedown in one quick movement. She prides herself on having the tax chart memorized.

She runs the check through the antiquated cash machine and calls goodnight. A brisk taxi smell blows across the bar as the couple exits to the quiet and snowy street. On the weekend, this corner is a crossroads of the world, but on weekday January nights, the quiet drifts.

"Jerry, you're here late. You off work tomorrow?"

"Yeah, taking a day off. They've got some event going on at the museum, and it's going to be a quiet day. I need to take care of some stuff I can never take care of on weekends."

Gus pushes his glass toward her and puts a cardboard coaster on top, indicating his imminent return. "I gotta run over to the facility. Be back soon."

Gus works at the NYU sports facility as the night manager. She calls him Gus the Drunk because that's what he calls himself. His father was a musician, and Louis Prima and other heroic jazz artists spent time in his childhood home.

Gus was an adult when he found out his grandfather was a made man. That opened up some other careers, along with a regular bender cycle. During one, he left a duffel bag at a bar down the street for two days. When he went to retrieve it, the bartender said, "I opened it up, saw about ten grand in cash with an axe on top of it, and I zipped it back up and waited for you to come back in."

Gus is loyal and always respectful of the girl as if she were his daughter.

"You ever need anything, a-n-y thing, you hear me, anyone gives you any trouble, I'll take care of it."

He rises, zips his jacket, pushes his chair in to the bar, steps out into the night. She watches him walk stiffly, head down. Memories of his cologne hang back.

"Gus has got the perfect job there." Jerry stubs out his cigarette neatly in the glass ashtray. It's about midnight, and she's happy it's just Jerry for a while.

He was her first friend in New York. Jerry is a painter in his late fifties, with a pleasant narrow face and a bald head ringed with soft gray hair. He went bald in his twenties, ". . . so it really was more of a novelty than anything, gave me plenty of time to accept that's how it was going to be.

Not like these guys with a full head of hair who freak out when they start losing it in their forties."

He is fastidious, kind, curmudgeonly, brilliant.

They have an easy way of being. She soaks up his Detroit history and finds it glamorous and funny. He never condescends to her, and she never holds anything back. They are real friends.

His greatest love is the tenor sax. He teaches her how to be a fan. She buys cassette tapes at his recommendation, plays them on the diner stereo throughout her shift. The nights spiral out in exquisite melody. Coltrane, Eddie Lockjaw Davis, Coleman Hawkins, Dexter Gordon, Sonny Rollins, Bill Perkins, Lester Young, then to Mingus and Monk and Red Garland, Oscar Peterson, and the singers—Dinah Washington, Blossom Dearie, Billy Eckstein, Ella. Jerry spills this knowledge, and she eats it up. He has an encyclopedic sort of mind, knows everyone who played on the records, every funny story of the musicians.

"Did I tell you the story of that time in Detroit when I saw Dinah Washington?"

"When she came barreling out of the bar and fired shots at a man across the street? So amazing!"

"I guess I did."

"I was listening to her today. I brought the tape back." She rustles in her bag under the bar and pulls the cassette out, walks over to the player and clicks it in. "Send Me To The 'lectric Chair" starts mid-song.

"Oh, you have to rewind it."

She does, and the tape starts with "After You've Gone." A couple of young men come into the restaurant and stand at the end of the bar. "You still serving food?"

"We are, have a seat." She brings menus and returns to the bar to pour glasses of water.

"I was telling someone today about going to see Johnny Griffin. God, that was a great night. 'I'll come meet the young lady!'" Jerry shakes his head and smiles at the memory.

She had paid for them to head over to the Village Vanguard to see Johnny Griffin. As a thank-you for all his information and his friendship, she dressed in her little red dress with the dice on it and set herself up.

This was a legendary night for them. Jerry had met Griffin previously and was tickled to show her this world. They sat at the bar rather than at a table because that's what musicians and people in the know did. Griffin was funny and self-deprecating and sexy in an old man sort of way. The music was challenging. She liked that. After the show, Jerry brought him over to meet her. They would speak of this for a long time.

"I loved that night! Let me take this order. I'll be right back."

The two men order burgers and fries. She hangs the check for the cook, who is sitting on a milk crate, reading a Chinese newspaper.

She steps back behind the bar. "I wish I could have seen Dinah in her heyday. Or Billie, or Ella. That would have been incredible."

"It was pretty great. I never saw Billie, but I saw Ella when she played in Detroit. Baker's Keyboard Lounge."

They converse this way for hours, for years. It amuses him to watch her struggle with the parade of heartbreaking humanity coming to drink at her bar. She gets in little dramas by extending herself, trying to help.

"When someone walks through the door and you feel sorry for them, just kick them out immediately. You're not strong enough," he advised.

Day in and day out, they spend hours together. Long history lessons of jazz and sometimes of physics, which he loves as well. She is a sponge.

The stories spin out and connect them. She speaks of her own upbringing sometimes. Who knows what Jerry makes of those stories. Once, when he was discussing baseball with another patron, she interjected. "That would be the infield-fly rule."

He fumed. "I could have been talking about baseball with you all this time?"

She would disappoint him later. The last time they would see each other, he was living under the Brooklyn Queens Expressway, in a dingy apartment dark with desperation. That is another story.

The bar changes temperature and Gus reenters, waving his hand as greeting. She dumps out the milky water in his glass and refills it.

"Everything all right over there, Gus?" Jerry greets him.

"Oh yeah, everything's fine. Looks like you're packing it up here soon?" He looks at the clock. One forty-five. She waves as the last customers leave.

"Yep, gotta start counting up. I am working breakfast tomorrow, so I'll be back at eight. Bartender switched her shift last minute and I'm stuck with it."

"You gotta be back here that soon?"

"Yeah, but then I have three days off. I might not leave my apartment the whole time."

"Well, I'll pack it up then. Have a nice few days off. Don't get into trouble." Jerry stands and puts his cigarette pack in his pocket. "See you this weekend."

"See you, Jerry. Have a good day off tomorrow."

She pulls the register drawer and begins to count while Gus finishes his drink. "Guess I'll go down the road and say hi there. You okay, want me to stay until you leave?"

"No, I'm okay Gus. Have a good night, see you this weekend."

The bar is quiet. She steps to the door, locks it, turns off the neon sign. She finishes her count and after preparing the morning register, wraps the cash in a tally sheet and leaves it for the owner to pick up in the morning. The cook lets her out the side door, and she hails a cab to her studio on Stanton Street between Attorney and Ridge. The regular pack of hooligans who sit on the steps of the building are absent. On a night like this she slips into the elevator and makes it to her apartment without incident.

There is urine sometimes in the corners of the elevator floor, and neighbors keep their doors open so kids can ride their Big Wheels up and down the hallway. It is loud, but her studio is fresh and clean, peaceful.

On her days off, there are long hours stretched out with just herself to account for. She has no television. She sits in an armchair and watches the sky change. Sometimes she worries about what is to come, about the path. Mostly, life is a moment-to-moment experience.

Who is that person, barely thinking of the future, living in the now?

She feeds the cat, washes her face and teeth and gets into bed, feeling the muscles of her legs popping and throbbing as they relax after the night on her feet.

She wakes four hours later, surprisingly refreshed. This is another gift given, the ability to greet every morning, song in heart, no matter the hours of sleep. She has yet to know how much use this will be later.

She throws on some clothes, says goodbye to the cat, glances at herself in the mirror and walks through the still and brightening streets to the restaurant. The owner greets her at the side door. "Back so soon?" He is a cheap motherfucker, but over the years she warms to him. He told her a story of his family's escape from mainland China, having to leave his infant sister behind. From then on, she cuts him a break. She is learning the world is wide. Heartbreak runs deep.

She opens a newspaper from the bodega next door and locates the crossword puzzle. Drinking tea, she puts her foot on the edge of the ice bin and starts in.

The diner wakes up around her. Customers straggle in, waitresses tell stories of their night. No one sits at the bar for a couple of hours, so she is free to do all three of the puzzles: the *Post*, the *Daily News,* the *Times.* She has a bagel and tea and chooses *Mingus Standards* for the stereo.

Tomorrow, the day off. She's dreaming of how she might spend it. If she wakes up early enough, maybe a stroll through the Lower East Side, reveling in the still faintly-felt past of Orchard Street shops and the Jewish neighborhood. Maybe hit Ratner's Dairy Deli for some blintzes. Maybe pull out the old Smith Corona.

Maybe this is how it will always be, she thinks.

April 8

just back from breakfast at ratner's dairy deli, sunday at
ratners and the whole lower east side seemed to be there. there
was a line nearly out the door and every table was taken except
for those in the back near the kitchen. i watched the kitchen
doors, the left side in and the right out, watched the parade of
waiters, most of them over sixty, grey and stooped. there were a
few young ones. young i mean thirty, and they seemed to feel they
were the hit of the show, walking very briskly and shouting to
each other little pep phrases. the busboys were all chinese,
walked with extremely fine posture, were all younger and neater
looking than most of the waiters. why were they chinese? i
could imagine once, in the twenties or thirties, someone, the
owners, deciding that the chinese were the hardest workers than
any other minority, and it has always stuck, the policy of the
chinese busboy. it is funny. the people at the take-out counter
are all women, all extremely over weight and baggy, their skin
hanging down in a pastry eating way. they wear blue, the
waiters and busboys all wearing ochre. the waiters wear dinner
jackets, the busboys in smocks.
so out of the right door of the kitchen came a contant parade of:
waiters with four coffee cups, their hands shaking as they set
down the cream, busboys, empty handed and bored looking, the women
in blue, with a pastry in each hand, kitchen help, chefs carrying
trays of white frosted cakes, or cheese balls, or boxes of fruit.
and it went on and on, until i felt that they would never stop,
that ratners stayed open forever, that the swinging doors was
someone's way of counting the seconds, minutes of this life. i
got the feeling that as long as the waiters and busboys and blue
women kept swinging through the doors that they would never die.
only get a little more bent as the years went by. a little more
wrinkled, a little slower. the chinese busboys, on the other
hand, would only get younger and porter, and better dressed, until
soon there would be such an exchange of power that the busboys
would be able to take over, leaving the others the grow slower and
slower and wither away to yellow dust along the path of the dining
room floor.
it is very surreal in ratner's.

24

There she is still, standing at the bar, doing puzzles. A couple of years older, her hair longer, a little more world about her. The morning turns into afternoon. An acquaintance sits at the bar, a man who owns a basement recording studio on Ludlow Street. He is from South America, exotic and funny. He speaks about the city and his studio and the music he makes.

"I'm learning to play the drums." She says it out loud to him, and I see the world pause. Light invades the windows and fills the restaurant and blinks with the shadows of bodies walking down Broadway.

Her boyfriend recently bought a hi-hat stand with cymbals, a snare drum and stand, and a kick pedal for ten dollars from a junkie friend who was paring down. The boyfriend fixes the kick pedal to a cardboard box, and in the afternoons she plays along to an Enigma record, learning simple patterns that repeat endlessly. She plays along to the Rolling Stones' "Sweet Virginia" to learn to shuffle.

At the bar, this announcement of her intent comes out of the blue, as a way to break up the sameness of the diner afternoon. There is Jerry, in the corner of the bar, reading a paper, coffee cup half-full. Gus will be here a little later, smelling of an old cologne whose strength tells us where in the bender cycle he is.

In a split second of fate, it occurs to her to see what happens when she says this from behind the bar, the bar that seems to deliver things she is looking for.

The man smiles and writes a number on a card. "Drums? Great! Here is the phone number of the best drum teacher in New York City."

Let's stop here. This is the moment I love to replay.

There it is, the card lilting across the bar to meet her outstretched hand. She won't remember that man's name, but she will remember his hand and the card in it that was to change everything.

My first drum lesson.

Fred sits me down at the drum set.

"Okay, now hit the drum."

I look at the snare drum. It shines vividly white, lit by the ceiling light of the basement studio. I gingerly pick up the drumsticks lying on the head and tap the drum politely.

He grabs the stick and laughs.

"No, I said HIT it." He smacks the stick on the drum, shattering the muffled quiet of the practice room. I jump. He lays the stick back into my hand.

I tighten up on it. I lift my arm. It is weighted by cobwebs of protocol that have ruled my life to this point, and as I tear through the heaviness, I hear voices: *Don't talk back! Quiet! Be nice! Children should be seen but not* . . . WHAM!

That snare drum hit signals the next chapter in my life, the one with drums in it. The chapter that brought me the real education: no money, crappy jobs, clinging to rent control, and an honest feeling of joy in any part of a day with drums in it. All day long on some.

The things I learned about myself while learning how to play an instrument far outweigh anything I learned on the kit. I found that my mind comforts itself with mathematics and that it always has. I found out that I see time as geometric shapes. I realized I have been counting to myself to alleviate stress since I was very young, hanging my feet over the end of my twin bed, counting and tapping as the terrors of the dark abound. I remembered that as a child I would do anything to be onstage. I connected to the fearlessness I thought had been lost through those teen years of curling back inside myself.

I was getting hung up by learning how to play the double-kick pedal. I had been reading and watching videos and getting the technique all tangled up in my head, so therefore I could barely work the thing at all.

I went to see the Melvins play a show and had a chance to speak with drummer Dale Crover afterward. I asked him about playing the double-kick pedal. I spouted a bunch of theories from what I had read.

Dale looked at me with a surprised smile. "There are no rules."

When I compare it to John Bonham's, the speed of my right foot will be an endless source of misery until the day I die. When I remember to treat it compassionately, this stubbornly resistant body part, I seem to have the most progress. I settle into training my foot the way I would a bumbling puppy, slowly and patiently and methodically. I let go of all my desires for the future, all regret of the past and for starting so late, and once again do very slow exercises. Sitting down to work is all that is required.

I'm not going to break any records today. I'm not going to set the world on fire with my kick drum technique this afternoon. Today, just do it for me. I sit down and do the work. As for the outcome, well, maybe next show I'll notice a difference.

We say we are too old to start something, and then we are too old to keep doing something. As someone who has been comfortably fixed in a childlike vision of reality for a long time, I wonder, to what relation of time are we speaking?

I feel the breath of the wind moving over the planet, watch the rise of tides, hear the thunder of waves breaking stone into tiny grains of sand that caress and hold us and will continue to cradle generations for as long as time. *There are no rules.* You get to go where your heart calls you.

You get to find joy in learning. You can find a teacher who makes you laugh, who says things in a way that helps a little wall in your mind dissolve, to reveal a truth about you that was hidden in plain sight.

26

"This was doubtless a premature satori, for I was unable to resist the temptation to write, think, and intellectualize about it. Yet when I am in my right mind I still know that this is the true way of life, at least for me."

~Alan Watts[8]

It has been thirty years since my first meditation retreat, during a blizzard in western Massachusetts. The storm cut the power and knocked down trees, and still the retreat went along, with little notes set around of how to do certain things, no sense of panic or worry.

I was gifted that first time with an experience of the falling away of separation. Maybe it was two seconds. Maybe it was an hour. The personality self dropped away and all was exquisitely one thing, one movement, one moment, one tone, one is, one it, One.

Words are so woefully inadequate in this description, and I see them there, on the page, and want to give up this conversation. I will forge on.

I explain this experience of realization by saying I was given something in order to set me on my way, on a path of spiritual exploration that brought me to today.

I had no framework for this experience. I had read one book about Zen meditation and stacks of literature hinting at such things: Salinger and Hesse and Jung. With no structure, I went along with the experience and figured everyone got to see something like that when they meditated so much. When I look at it now, I remember how deeply familiar this glimpse was, like something I already knew.

The joy that arose did not go away, ever. The manic part of it lasted several months. A couple of weeks after my return, I tried to work, as a document specialist in an investment bank. I got sent home. They thought I was on drugs.

One of the things that happened was my eyes opened and stayed open, with the sense that I wasn't just seeing from the pupil but from the whole eye, lid to lid and corner to corner. I don't think I was blinking much. I felt I had never looked anyone in the eye. Now when I spoke to someone, the connection radiating eyeball to eyeball was as though the energy of the other self poured into me as we spoke.

That direct staring doesn't make people uncomfortable, not at all.

I remember standing on a train, crammed into the subway in the normal way, and looking at a man's neck, the little hairs and blemishes, falling so in love with the sweetness and vulnerability of it that I started to openly weep. I saw an older European man struggling to make a phone call in Grand Central Station, so I paid for his call and walked him to his hotel.

Obviously, this way of being was not conducive to living in the city, but also, where better to be a lunatic. I kind of fit right in.

I have had similar experiences of opening since then, but none as disruptive. Here, I will write more metaphors of this unexplainable thing in insufficient language.

I dropped through a thin barrier in my mind and found vast and exquisite truth. It was just on the other side, right there for me to see. If I turned my awareness down a different hallway, the world came rushing in and rushing out at the same time. The motion was of a flower infinitely opening and closing, and in that opening was everything that has ever been, one moment and yet perpetual movement outside of time. It was a dropping away of all knowing and a knowing of everything as one thing. In fact, there was no "knower," just the known. The aliveness of everything was a fundamental part of it, and the world became completely animated, whereas before it was like cardboard, rigid. Here in this reality was everything and nothing. And beyond all that, the feeling of being profoundly loved.

I was filled with a joy that enlivened everything I saw. The joy is still here, it has always been here. There were times over the years when I could not access it. Years when I resisted it. The darkest times were when I believed this experience had been a mistake, a fluke, and I was unworthy of ever knowing this truth again. If I had framed it as seeing God, in these dark times I would have said I thought God had forsaken me. It didn't matter the words used; it was the same feeling. Despair developed by believing that my young, ignorant, unknowing self had stumbled into truth. This had been an accident, a mistake, a cosmic error that had allowed me into the VIP section where I had no business being.

As a child, I had to figure out how to rein in my innate joyfulness in order to function in the world, as most of us do, and this served me well as I went back to my life and functioned. Here is a great ignorance, to believe it is necessary to cultivate cynicism, to cut off the gifts of buoyancy and light in order to conduct ourselves. There was always a fear of losing connection with normal reality, so I pushed away the gift of being in order to live my life.

When I returned from the retreat, I felt a kind of newness, finding my way into every movement as if it were the first time, blinded by the light in all and baffled that others couldn't see it. I would roll it over, try to explain it, to describe it. There were moments when someone would ask about my trip, and I would regale them with the information of what I had seen. I would try to explain, but the conversations always left me feeling ill, as if by speaking of the experience I negated it. As I explained it in words, I seemed to diminish it, and gradually, I pushed it further away with the belief that I was unworthy of it.

Over time I developed a strong feeling of the experience having been a mistake, that I had been chosen by accident to see what I saw. This sense of "not enough" amplified the lack that already existed and rang through the years.

I began the chase, thinking I should have a similar experience every time I sat in meditation. Craving causes suffering. It can happen with meditation as much as it can happen with cookies. This has been a subtle challenge, like trying not to think of an elephant when someone says, "Don't think of an elephant." Knowing this experience is possible means that some days, all I do is work to detach myself from the longing for the same kind of connection.

Accepting, receiving what is, not judging anything as better or worse, this is the answer. To realize that this experience was not "better" than any other I have had is to snap all the cables that elevate the ideal.

Along with feeling unworthy then is spending time judging the experience. This is where the intellectual pursuit propelled through all these years became dangerous. *This* other writer had a similar experience, but *they* had energy flowing through their physical body while it happened to them. *This* person devoted their life to spiritual practice from that moment on. *That* person became a saint. *This* person a teacher. I am not reading enough, or practicing enough, or maybe I am reading too much or doing wrong practice.

Here it comes again, the self-judgment and the feeling of "not enough." Geez, it never ends.

Actually, it does end. It ends by finding an open awareness of Now, where all beings and all moments are equally loved. The ego tries to control that which is beyond. The ego tries to understand, to explain, to work toward, to diminish, to get the experience back, when the ego has nothing at all to do with this. The heart is where knowing lives.

THE ROVER

27

"The Rover" is my favorite Led Zeppelin song to play. It is my warm-up song, the first one I learned. I get this song. There is a magic pattern hidden in Bonham's grooves, an implied syncopation that comes in and out of a drummer's awareness. It is the most delicious feeling possible to uncover it. I find it here.

This song is my natural tempo. I feel that good when I play, like falling into a warm pool just a bit warmer than you are.

I love the words of this song, the mini travelogue. I love the feeling of futility, the search for what is meaningful, the longing for home. I love how I lift into the sky during the big part in the middle. I love how Bonham brings us back to that funky little pattern at the end. I love the sexiness, placed oh so right in space and time. You must channel the relaxation and authority essential to a song like this for it to be right.

Any song that requires me to stomp on the hi-hat is a favorite. When I sit to play drums, I sit with my thighs parallel to the ground, maybe a little higher than parallel. Then it is easy to stomp, to lift my whole leg and let it fall. Those upbeat hits on the splayed-open cymbals give the band a wet shove.

After sound check, you think you know what things will be like at the dive into the first song of the set, but you can't be certain. Several hours have probably passed since you set everything up. If it is a rental kit, it's a crapshoot whether it will feel okay during the show. Sometimes, after the first few measures of that first song, the realization dawns that you will be conducting battle for the next two hours.

When you set up the drums, you might have just driven all day. There might be problems with the way the drums are arranged and you think, *Eh, too much trouble to fix. I can live with it.* That "fix it later" attitude is going to screw you, little missy.

Screw you, it shall. The bass drum slides. The hi-hat walks. The sound of the snare in the monitor is ridiculous, and you can't hear the guitar. The clutch on the hi-hat gives way, and now there is no opening or closing the thing, so your whole attention is brought to the tip of the stick, trying to play near the bell to not drown out the vocals. The crash cymbal pulls away with each hit. The floor tom bites your knuckle.

Drumming is about millimeters. A cymbal or snare drum a little too close or a little too high can stop the flow. Injury happens by slamming fingers on equipment I didn't expect to be so close. I reach to crash on the cymbal, and I miss it entirely and hit only air, or worse, a metal protrusion I didn't expect to be there. I drop a stick.

Meanwhile, what better song in which to experience all this? Remember that warm pool? Just stay in comfort and anything that happens is just some splashing on the surface. The song plays itself. It can't help but play. We don't lose the one, we don't enter a section incorrectly, we don't fuck up the form. The ship is traveling, baby, staying right in its lane, collecting information about what should be adjusted when it docks.

My band rocks this song. In the first few notes, I see performance fall on them, transform them. I see them arrive, step to the front of the stage and deliver. After this song, no one should be in question that their money will be worth it. We turn on the ignition, and sometimes the engine takes a moment to warm up, but if it does, by the time we hear her sing about joining hands, the motor is purring and we are all together here.

28

Around the side of the restaurant, on Bleecker Street, was an unmarked door and a staircase down. This was the entrance to the basement pool hall, the hidden bar beneath the diner. There were three pool tables down there, a jukebox, and a long bar. It was always dark. It smelled moldy and old. The owner locked the door that led up to the kitchen when her shift started. The only way out was across the bar and up the stairs. This worried her some.

The patrons for the most part were quiet and funny men who played pool with concentration and no joy.

"If there's a fight, just kneel down back there behind the bar. No need to worry about it. Just duck." She was told this early on, but the only fight she witnessed was between two women, one a great pool player who riled it up down there, igniting a kind of electricity when she was playing.

The girl behind the bar, she was more of a calming element. She befriended the men, listened to their stories, sat through the tedious nights of pool playing. They tried to teach her pool, but she was an erratic player. She would run the table when she first picked up the cue, and then for the rest of the night her mind would enter the game, and she wouldn't be able to get a single ball sunk.

"She may be beautiful, but she plays pool worth shit," was announced to the tables one night. After that, she stopped trying to play and just sat behind the bar, and read, and listened to stories.

The jukebox was across the bar, and a big man shaped like Humpty Dumpty would come there often to play it. There was something different about his brain. He would pull out a train schedule and ask her the same question every time, worded exactly the same, not care about receiving an answer, buy a coke, tip a dime. Then, he would go to the jukebox and play James Brown's "Sex Machine," stand in the corner, and dance, which would entail standing in one place and rocking his big round belly up and down, his belt cutting across his midsection. It was comical, but she was gravely protective of him. After he had played the song five or six times, the pool players would yell at him to knock it off. He would look startled, pick up his bag, head up the stairs. She would have let him play that song all night if he wanted. She could listen to the same song into infinity, and it seemed to please him so much.

It was around 2:00 a.m., a weekend night. There were still people there, so she was going to be there until four, pouring drinks and listening. Gil was an acquaintance from the bar. Tall and thin with dark curly hair, bedroom eyes, and always with a hat. He had grown up in the wilds of Canada. His father had fallen out of a plane and survived, taking this as a sign he should start his own religion. Gil grew up with his birth mother and a few other mothers living on the property with them, and his childhood consisted of escaping the home for long walks through the woods with his dog, who saved his life once from a wolf or a bear. Gil was a genius with electronics and had the withdrawn and soft exterior of a man who spent a lot of time alone.

This night, he comes down with some friends from a studio where he is wiring a recording console. One of those men is to become her partner for the next twelve years.

At this point, anyone with a career seems glamorous to her, and Greg's job seems extra glamorous. He is the studio engineer in a recording studio across from the police station in Chinatown.

She feels his interest immediately. Later she would realize that this interest applied to most attractive women, and that would drive her crazy. But here, now, she was in love with the way he looked at her, as if she were the center of everything.

He told her he would come see her the next time she was working, and she waited for him all night. She was just ending her shift when he came in, out of breath. He had run through the streets to get to her.

They went back to the recording studio that night, and this began an education in music and recording that has carried her through to this day. How generous he was with his knowledge, with his love of sound. They would lie talking until the sun came up, speaking of the movement of sound from speaker to ear drum, or dissecting the magic of other recordings.

He would work for days at a time. After sessions with clients, he would engineer his own music. His talent for rhythm and songwriting and engineering dazzled her. She would pull a baffle down and find an equipment blanket, lie on the floor while he worked, watching him turn buttons, trying to hear how the changes he made affected the sound. The way to edit was to cut the two-inch tape with a razor blade, and she watched as he listened for the beginning and end of a sound to hear where to cut.

It was in this studio that words started to rise when she was listening to music. She would write while he was working, and the connection of music and words created a hunger inside of her. Gradually, they began writing together, he adding music to her words and vice versa. Then, she tried her hand at singing and fronting a band. Then, she chose drums.

There was no one else who could have been more encouraging as she picked her way through understanding the possibilities of her life in music. He saw the positive in everything she did and was deeply supportive. There was a magic in how they communicated, and when she was learning to play drums, his instruction turned on lightbulbs. They started to play together. Any suggestion he made about a drum pattern was instantly understood, and she could do it.

This is how music took her over. This is a story of two great loves. One lasted, the other fell apart, another terrible ending to a relationship, as was her pattern. If he were to know how much gratitude for his light she carries with her in every song, how his humor and brilliant wisdom and pure heart influences every drumbeat, he might forgive her just a bit.

29

I sit on the airplane next to a tall, thin young man with narrow wrists and a nose that hints at having been raised well and thoughtfully. His skin is poreless, this much I can see. He orders a burger from the United cart and eschews the bun, taking big gobbly bites that say eating is something he wishes he didn't have to do, that he is embarrassed to partake. I imagine he wants to get back to his device, a device of a size that tells me I know nothing of the ocean of possibilities in technology. It sits before him on the tray. He keeps his hands in his lap, his body so straight and yet comfortable and still, and I think, *This younger generation. There is so much they know that I don't.*

I have some drink coupons, so I order Canadian Club, two please, and 7UP. The young man watches the small brown bottles handed over him with a vague interest he is too polite to make obvious. I bring to mind all the writers and actors I look up to. I imagine how they would charm the steward into giving them more than their due, but that's not me, here, back in steerage.

The conversation is brusk. I speak steadily and directly when I order because I am not immune to the youth's judgment. He knows more at his young age about nutrition and work ethic and probably spiritual growth than I knew then or may ever know, but I order cocktails like a boss.

I know the path of enlightenment is one of contradiction, and this personality of mine has its heroes: Bukowski, Bacon,

Richards, Watts. The futility of living for the future burns deep in me. I can't help but order the drinks.

The flight is four hours. I have been frustrated to not have had time to write for many days. A membrane has grown over my mind, a thick membrane made of blood and voices that tell me that nothing I write or say will matter. The CC&7 will lubricate it, tease it into suppleness, and with luck, break it open.

My use of this metaphor says the cocktail is working already.

All the shades in the airplane are closed, but I say fuck it. I douse the row of the aircraft with white light as I crack open heaven. I want to see clouds. The formations outside are so majestic I hear "Ave Maria," and my heart sings with the beauty of it. I will never get over flying. I will never get over the wonder of layers of cloud banks and the way the land is laid out in squares and hieroglyphics, and how some genius figured out how to transport bodies through the air. Earlier, the clouds were arranged in a graph, dollops of white set out in perfect rows and with a mathematical arrangement so precise it was hallucinatory.

Now, the clouds are cappuccino foam. The formations are so deep and stunning I completely forget they mean storms. I can look right down into a cocoon of white, and I think, *Please, let me one day fall into those secret heavenly blue hollows. Let them catch me.*

30

How many shows have I played for no one? Or I should say, for the bar staff and, if lucky, for the other bands?

How many excuses have I heard over the years for the lack of attendance? *There is a big event in town taking people away from our show. There is an article in the local paper about gang violence at the venue. The sports team is in the playoffs, and everyone is at the bar up the street because they have television. No one knows the promoter, or he's pissed people off, or he's on drugs, or he has no idea what he's doing.* The wan faces of the bartenders hint at secret stories of drama and corruption. *It's a beautiful day, and everyone wants to be outside. It's a rainy/ snowy/steamy day, and everyone wants to be anywhere but here.*

As a musician, you can't help but develop an ability to accept your fate. We load into a venue, a big, echoey, concrete place. The minutes click by, we get closer to set time, and it begins to dawn on us: there is not going to be anyone here.

We start giving each other ironic, bemused looks. Each time the front door opens, our heads turn in anticipation, as if we're waiting for a busload of rockers, ready to party. After a while, hope escapes the room. We go from anticipation to resignation to a kind of giddiness at the ridiculousness of giving a party for no one.

Rule of thumb: you play as if there are three hundred people there. Always and without question. First, because that's what you're getting paid for (if you're lucky), but second and most important, because this is what you do. This is what every moment of your life leading up to this point has been for. All the lessons and practicing and travel and money spent, this is what it's for. You get to play your instrument. You get to play with the people onstage. Your whole life is for the love of it, and this minor annoyance of the empty venue is par for the course.

We always say, *Well, it's a paid practice.* But when the music starts it never feels like practice. It's the real thing no matter who is there.

You close your eyes and revel in your instrument. You have fun onstage with your bandmates, maybe attempt some moves you would be intimidated to debut in front of people. You listen closely to the songs and try out approaches you always wanted to try. You put on a great show. There is no other option.

Never mind that at such a performance, playing to ten people, one of the ten hired my band to perform on a nationwide tour. Things like that have happened one, maybe two times in all the shows in all the empty venues. You can think, *Well, you have to give it your all since you never know who will walk in that door.*

That remote possibility is not what it is about.

You get to play. That's it.

The last note ripples into the big, empty room like a dying thunderclap. The house music comes on after a pregnant pause, like titters of rain after the storm. You laugh, you pack your stuff, you chalk it up.

Rule of thumb: always grateful.

31 A week before an important show, I can start to obsess. I want the night to be great from beginning to end, and a week away I start to get plagued by worry.

When I get really wound up about it, I have a few techniques to bring me back to earth. First, I imagine the worst-case scenario:

> Saturday night, no one will show up.

> Or, people will show up and my equipment will fail me.

> Or, my equipment will work but I will forget how to play.

> Or, I will play the show and everyone will see what a terrible drummer I actually am.

> Or, I will play the show and only thirteen people will be there to see it. Career over.

> Or, I will never get to play the show because I die.

> Or, the show will never happen because everyone dies.

Somehow, this calms me down. When I spin out the worst-case scenario to the most extreme conclusion, it starts to put things in perspective. Really? The show is that important? EVERYONE COULD DIE.

I am not sure why this is comforting.

Another technique I find helpful is to look at this picture I keep of the space shuttle leaving Earth.

NASA May 16, 2011

The futility of the image makes me feel so tender about our minuscule acreage in the vastness of the universe. Look at that little spaceship. Look at the enormity of a planet hanging so small in the echoes of space. It breaks my heart to think of our marvelous self-absorption.

Finally, the real help comes from the technique of finding the quiet place lying within me, beneath this Clementine who walks the planet with all her emotions and thoughts and fears and anticipation. I see I understand nothing of the forces at work since before I was born to create her. I understand that I understand nothing, but I know.

From this knowing, my upcoming show comes into view. I am onstage, behind my drums, looking out on an audience of people who paid to see my band play. I see the women in my band with their instruments; I feel how much I adore them. I see us creating spirals of sound reaching across the decades to bring forth the whispers of ancestors.

And rock.

32

A weekend in the Midwest. An unease settled on me, and I felt myself raw and overly sensitive to the slights of others. Maybe it had to do with the heat and humidity of the summer weather, or maybe I had been alone too much, the shock of socializing jarring.

Whatever the reasons, I started to fixate on the annoyances. Sub-par backline equipment. The basement dressing room, sweaty and smelling as if a gas generator was pumping fumes through the rooms. Maybe it was because each performance would be a struggle to play on rented drum kits, since I had flown to the shows instead of driving my equipment. Maybe it was the rude customer at the rental-car place, or the loud ten-year-olds and even louder mother behind me on the flight, or the stopped traffic from St. Louis to Illinois.

Things started to annoy me, and aggravation built up. Rather than follow my own advice and observe my reactions, I let everything fester. Venue personnel barked orders instead of making requests. A fan shouted at me to come speak to him at a table, yelling rudely as if summoning a waitress. A man refused to listen to me when I explained—six times—that the reason I couldn't shake his hand was because mine had been blister-bloodied during the show. And, annoyance of all annoyances, someone told me to smile.

I got tired of being bossed around. I felt my skin bristling as I encountered anyone, no matter how friendly or how kind. The small muscles in my shoulders pulled themselves into a protective shell, and my arms ached holding back a desire to throw elbows. I was physically on high alert, not only anticipating the next insult but also actively watching for it. Then, I started to berate myself as smiling people, whom I had been so happy to see, said hello, and I couldn't muster graciousness.

The next step was to take every insult out to the global, as if my injuries needed to be justified and amplified by a broader conspiracy. My mind groused that my friends in all-male bands don't get bossed around as much. They weren't expected to be polite and entertaining constantly. The female band gets the crappy gear. The female band doesn't get paid the same. The female band has to give and give and give, working harder and harder for less. I doused the fire with more fuel, the flames higher, the thinking more exaggerated and angrier.

This progressed to an internal self-abasement. Now, I was misery, as raw and sore as my hands became each night in the wet heat, sloughing off their blisters mid-set and bleeding on the drumsticks. Every slight was recorded, and my skin crawled in anticipation of the next offense. Then, I started looking for the next irritation to justify my bad mood.

A battle raged, back and forth between the frustration I was feeling, and then talking myself out of my feelings. *Maybe I'm just tired. Maybe I didn't meditate enough in the morning. Maybe I've reached my limit of the constant "on" that is required.* Then I turned to an easy target: finances, that most worldly of manifestations I desperately try never to stress over.

But finances loomed large in my head: the dragging along, the eking out, the barely subsisting, the amount of pushback that comes from venues and promoters and everyone's miserly ways. In the airless, overheated greenroom I lay on the floor, since there are never enough couches in these places—yet another annoyance!—and I questioned if this is really what I am supposed to be doing. I imagined giving up, where I would go, what I would do, what life would be without this bottomless pit of struggle that is the life of a musician.

My bandmates make the best of all situations, and I began to cogitate how much luckier they would be without me. All the ways I fail them ran like credits to a movie in my mind. They could find a better drummer, a better band, a better bandleader, a better friend. After each show I longed to crawl away, leave the celebration to the women and the fans, and not have my shadow cast misery on their light. Instead, I forced myself to socialize and inflicted myself—a grouchy, petulant participant—on everyone I met.

I hid in the greenroom, trying to distract myself with something other than my own life, and, as a kind of self-flagellation, read a *New Yorker* article about the Syrian revolution. The story was hopeful and then despairing. So much suffering going on, right now, and here I am in a ridiculous life bitching about frivolous things.

The despair was now complete. Not only was my life misery but also useless and wasteful. I retreated into a small burrow of darkness as the pain body moved through loading equipment and checking into hotel rooms and the rest of it. Sleep was the only refuge, until the bright light through the hotel curtains blasted the room too early. The final nail.

This is all difficult to write because it is probably apparent I adore my music career. I enjoy the people who attend the shows and support the band, and I am beyond grateful for being able to play music for a living and for people who attend the shows and support my creative process. I am grateful for my band and for my ability and for the people who work so hard to create a night of entertainment and creativity and magic for others.

There is always more work to do. I have sat in meditation for thirty years, witnessing these patterns of thought and emotion and getting right into the muck and mire to investigate the tendencies of my human condition. Yet still, a weekend comes along, and it is as if none of that work has been for any good. There are still times I get swallowed up in these fires of delusion. I still forget I have the ability to erase misery in any moment by clearing the lens of perception and creating a new reality for the next moment.

Why allow myself to get so carried away? Maybe there is something I find difficult to see, so my small self creates a big smoke screen of a bad mood to avoid the real work. Maybe when I am uncomfortable, it is better to reach for the familiar instead of meeting the situation in a new way. Maybe I am too vulnerable. Maybe there is still so much of this personality self I feel needs to be defended.

Drums gifted me with moments of forgetting, onstage. Yet again, this dear love washed away the misery as I played. Behind the drums on the last night, I saw how we create our reality, and how we are creating together. I am an invention of everyone in the room.

I let my mind open and imagined being guided by what the audience wanted to see. There was no Clem and no petulant grump. There was no one there who would later write how challenging the weekend was, how challenging the job. There was only physical form propelling sound and joyful waveforms moving through bodies and hearts, into ears, for everyone who wanted to hear.

As I played, I saw how much of my personality was reinforced by fear, and separateness, and buying into a culture and mindset that wants me to lose faith in the big picture. That which is untouched rose as I played.

I could settle back into my own darkness when I left the stage if I chose. I saw how I was choosing it. This is a kind of wallowing, to be shown the light and decide to go back to the darkness. I kindly accepted that the small self still, after all this time, needed its wallow.

Whether it is a bad mood we set up to prove from the beginning, or a bad mood we dive into like an ever-deepening well, it is something we choose. The constant work is to be present when making our choices. Which apparently is a lifetime of work, I once again discovered.

33 My breath is uneven, my heart a little faster than usual. On a three-day weekend of shows, this is natural. I am driving and loading the van and having fun with the band, meeting people and seeing friends, and in meditation I see the enervation. My adrenal system kicks in. I observe it, resting here in the quiet beneath it all.

How delicate we are. The busy weekend, with the extra physical exertion, the additional human contact, the lack of sleep, creates chaos in the physical body. My breathing is shallow, as if I'm panting. My muscles are held tense, and I seem unable to release them. Deep down there is a clenching and tightness fatiguing to hold and impossible to let go. I get tired making such an effort to hold myself together.

In meditation, I observe my muscles, tightly diligent. As I breathe, they release little by little. My blood seems to wash easier through my body with the relaxation that comes with breath. My thoughts, running nonstop, keep running, but I don't follow as closely anymore. I see them up there, on the surface, as I sink below, as if I am sinking to the bottom of a sea. It is a wide sea of awareness—peaceful, still, quiet.

I play a game in which I sink beneath the sounds in my environment: the slam of hotel doors, voices of the cleaning crew, the hum of the building. Beneath sound is another sound, a kind of white noise lying quietly underneath. As I find that frequency, I follow it deeper into the stillness of consciousness, and rest.

34

A monk decides to meditate alone, away from his monastery. He takes his boat out to the middle of the lake, moors it there, closes his eyes and begins his meditation.

After a few hours of undisturbed silence, he suddenly feels the bump of another boat colliding with his own. With his eyes still closed, he senses his anger rising, and by the time he opens his eyes, he is ready to scream at the boatman who dared disturb his meditation. But when he opens his eyes, he sees it's an empty boat that had probably got untethered and floated to the middle of the lake.

At that moment, the monk achieves self-realization, and understands that the anger is within him; it merely needs the bump of an external object to provoke it out of him.

From then on, whenever he comes across someone who irritates him or provokes him to anger, he reminds himself, "The other person is merely an empty boat. The anger is within me."

~Chuang Tzu

In a ten-day meditation retreat, I roomed with seven or eight other women. The accommodations were simple, low wooden bed frames with single mattresses on which to put a sheet and sleeping bag.

When you take a vow of silence, this doesn't mean only speech. It means gesturing too. Living with a group of people, you learn to wait. Someone in your way? You wait. You don't make your needs known in any way. You wait. Your perception of others becomes heightened so as to not bother them or take them out of their bubble.

The thing I feared most was that I would thoughtlessly jar someone out of their inner work. I trod lightly all day, and as the retreat progressed, I became an island of solitude in a room full of other solitudes.

There was one woman of whom I was very aware the whole time. She was small and loud. She had a stompy way of walking, and she seemed to hurl her body into bed, causing it to rattle against the wall. She would rifle through her duffle each morning and night, frantic and chaotic. Everything she did seemed to draw attention to herself.

During those nine days of silence, a good part of my time was spent thinking about this person. We didn't get much of a chance to meet people before the call to silence, so I hadn't spoken to her before. I imagined her voice loud and abrasive, cutting into conversations and opinionated. I could not for the life of me imagine what someone like her would be doing here. She must be going crazy in the silence, I thought, being so self-centered and immature. I considered what she did for a living, what her voice sounded like, issues we might argue about.

Basically, of this precious time when I was privileged to live the contemplative life of a monk, some of it was spent hating on this chick.

On the last day of the retreat, when the final instruction came and we headed to the cafeteria to break the silence, everyone's mouth started babbling a million miles an hour. I happened to have the good fortune to sit next to this person, my nemesis.

Up close, her skin was that creamy color that pairs with most redheads. She had a captivating light to her face. We started speaking, and she was gentle, sweet, humble, and funny. She worked with homeless people and was getting a master's degree in social work.

We spoke, and after a while she turned to speak to someone else. I sat quietly for a moment and allowed the realization to dawn on me. *Oh!* I thought.

I'm *the asshole!*

Here I was spending time I could have been spending on becoming one with the divine, and instead my ego was dumping its own judgments and insecurities and self-centeredness on this delight of a human.

Here I was, putting negativity into this boat, and at the end of the day it had absolutely nothing to do with the boat. It was all me, baby. All that junk was just a big old barge of Clem ugliness.

As we go through the world, the mind is constantly judging, looking backward to see how now compares, looking forward to anticipate what might come. Each moment is judged by past or future, every being judged according to others we have experienced. We always wish everything to be different than it is and compare everything to what once was.

I am reminded of this when I walk into a business and step up to the counter, look the attendant in the eye, and speak directly and clearly about what I have come to purchase. Nine times out of ten, the person will ask me to repeat what I've said. I know they've heard me. I know they were looking at my mouth move and that I was enunciating clearly. I also know they were not present for the first request. They were in the past, or in the future. They seem to be here, but some memory, some judgment, some emotion has blurred their vision, taken them away from the moment. I guess this is why eyewitnesses often have differing ideas of an event. It is a rare person who is right here, right now.

We also love to manufacture our reality from our past experience. How many times have I created a phony personality out of a musician's performance? How many times have I created a whole persona for someone as I watch them sing or play, only to discover later they are the opposite of what I had dreamed? I can see all my own desires and needs and preferences in this false creation. Later, backstage, when I see what I believe is the reality of the offstage persona, I know this too is a judgment, a creation.

At the retreat, I assumed so much about the woman I was rooming with. When I heard her walk down the hall, memories flooded my brain of all the people I have known who walked loudly. I was never seeing her. I was seeing decades of reactions to situations real and imagined. Those reactions clouded my vision, created a reality that was all mine.

What if on the last day, all my ideas about this woman had been true? What if she had been self-centered and ignorant? Then, I would have thought I was seeing confirmation, but really, it would have been a confirmation of my own preferences and beliefs. I would still not be seeing the real person. The point is that it doesn't matter how the other person appears. My reaction creates my reality.

Without story and without judgment, experience devoid of reaction is pure. I ask, *Who is experiencing?* I see very clearly the Clem who judges and craves for things to be different.

There is the story of the Buddha, sitting under the tree, saying, *Forget it. I'm sitting here until I finally understand reality.* What is the reality he studied? The only reality anyone truly knows: sensations of the body. Everything beyond the body is suspect, after all. Are we being dreamed by some big entity? Are we a hologram? A mirror? All we know is our reactions, reactions rising in the physical body, which are connected to our thoughts and emotions and manifesting in reaction to external stimuli.

The Buddha sat and observed these reactions and the *sankharas* being created. Sankharas are the deep, dug-in attachments to our experiences. When the Buddha let go of these reactions, he released the sankharas. He declared he finally understood reality. He understood that to let go of our reactions and judgments is to live in the true light of being.

If I had been truly aware in that retreat, if I had found unconditional conscious awareness and had experienced clarity in my moments, then where is judgment? There would have been a joy in each sound experienced, joy for being alive in the moment, and love for every stompy reverberation ringing forever. The boat would have been bumped, and there would be no boats, no bumps, just the delight of a river sighing.

MOBY DICK

There is a voice inside me. Most days, it seems as if there are many voices, darting in and out, ideas rising and falling in an inner conversation. At a silent meditation retreat, after three and a half days these inner voices converge into one big megaphone in the center of my head, each thought as clear as if someone were speaking them into my ears.

When it became apparent I could listen to my thoughts this way, as one big thought, I noticed how much of what I was listening to was an attack, a denigration, of Clem.

How loud these attacks became when I agreed to do the Moby Dick drum solo.

I haven't been playing long enough.

Drum solos are embarrassing. I like hearing a drummer play a song, not show off. No one wants to hear it.

Too old. Too fat.

You can't practice a solo, it has to be spontaneous. The audience has to journey with you from confidence to second-guessing to joy and abandon. This means you will really fuck up, lose your train of thought, never find the groove. You will be humiliated in front of an audience, in front of your band.

Too inexperienced. I am no (insert drum-mer name here).

I know zero licks. I am a lazy jerko who never commits and never practices and You Suck.

Give up. No one wants what you got.

Waste of space. Not good enough. Give up.

Somewhere beneath the thoughts lay other things. Some of the careless innocence that drew me to drums in the first place rose.

Once, a therapist guided me to envision the self who smoked. I saw my twenty-one-year-old self, in a crop top and teased hair, slouched in a corner and flipping the world off. That "go fuck yourself" energy may be a saving grace in my life, even though the smoking had to go.

I committed to do the solo. All I could do was my best and offer my effort as a gift.

If my performance is a gift I offer, I do my best to spend time playing from inside my heart in order to express my love for this instrument, these songs, this place and time, the lis-tener. A gift given. If the audience doesn't accept it, then they can find what they're looking for elsewhere. Their journey is not mine to take on.

What if the solo is an opportunity for prayer? If I find the center of my physical body, move from my spine, the body becomes its own animal and reaches for patterns aligned with heart. I sink into gratitude for movement and thus ignite a conversation with the divine.

That is the formula for the solo I offer: physicality plus gratitude equals joy. This desire to offer joy as a gift is what propelled me to agree.

It has never been right. I have never accomplished the transcendence I feel in my soul. My chops-building is so slow, and I fight a crippling feeling of defeat when I hear Bonham's live versions. I am always searching for a way to draw the audience into the drums, onto the drums, propelling movement and dancing and abandon, and I never reach them the way I want. I must try and not try, work hard and effortlessly play. There is a river I am to flow with, and continually I face-plant on the sandy shoal.

Yet, when I am in it, I connect with a fearlessness that allows me, in the moment, to just go. The voice quiets, the drums speak only. The very concept of mistake dissolves until the final hit of the song, when I must stand and bow, no matter how much humiliation cascades and drapes over me, shroud-like, as I do. While I am in it, the internal tirade goes away. Joy reigns.

36

I wake in the center of a hot flash. Heavy on the mattress, my back and the back of my neck and head are slick and sweaty. I've thrown off the sheet in my sleep, and the front of my body is exposed to heavy dark air. There is a first awareness, not so much language as feeling. A feeling moving from the base of my throat to my pelvis, an aching realization of thickness, of heaviness. A gray fog of shame settles around my core. There is a fire hose lodged in my side, pumping dense gray ash into the center of myself. I can't get under this gray, as I am too far inside of it, and it is too familiar to block or plug up or stop from happening.

The first real thoughts, once the mind crawls back into language and the awareness of my skin and limbs wakes, are of diet.

A panicking stream of ideas floods my head: if I don't eat anything all day, how quickly will I start to feel weight dropping off. No, I can't not eat, or the body goes into starvation mode and no weight will come off. I'll eat an apple for breakfast, maybe one egg. Poached to get the full benefit. First, I'll go running, that's the key. Exercise! I will get out there as soon as the sun comes up, since I'm frightened these days of heading out to the waterfront in the dark. I'll run, or do my best, since my knees and ankles and feet are in pain when I run. Then, I'll come home and do crunches and push-ups and planks and squats. Then, I'll go play drums, vigorously, for at least two hours. Then, yoga.

I think of seeing my yoga teacher after not taking a class for a month, and the shame fog tightens and constricts around the center of me. I can't tell how much weight I've gained in the month I've been away, but I am sure he'll see it, sure he'll notice. Can I just stay in the house for at least a week until I lose ten pounds? Can I exercise constantly and eat, what should it be, eight hundred calories a day? I think that will keep the metabolism going, the little metabolism I have left after a lifetime of this way of being.

A lifetime of this way of being. I think of Patti Smith. Not once in her books have I come across any mention of her physical self, of thinking about the way she looks other than to describe a haircut or outfit. The shame cloud becomes an ache through my body. This makes me so sad. All this thought and feeling around such nonsense. Now, I am trivial too.

When I think about it, my body is miraculous. Thank God for such health, such hale and powerful lungs and heart and muscles. I can stand and look in the mirror and feel this way for an instant. But then, as I focus in on the true picture, I can barely look. The skin is beautiful, I can see that. But the thighs are hanging and riddled with cellulite. The arms have cellulite on the upper part and are huge and unpleasant. The midsection is round and sticking out. I wish for money for colonics and then battle out the benefits of them in a circular thought that swirls around like water in a bowl heading down. Then the shoulders, raised and powerful from years of drumming, which shortens the neck. I look like a fifty-year-old woman around the bottom of the chin. I despair.

I think of Patti again. All the wasted time. This makes me angry. All the energy thinking of my body and my diet and my shame. This isn't even mine. I know I am responding to a programming from culture. What could I have accomplished without this pattern, this contraction of self-attack so familiar it is hard to imagine a different way of being?

None of the internal dialogue stops when I'm thin. Then, the window of what is proper behavior gets narrower. I think constantly of how to stay thin, worry about everything that goes in my mouth, not going out into the world from day-to-day due to even small fluctuations in my weight. It is the same no matter what weight I am at. It is the same.

In truth, I have stopped experience because of this shame. I have neglected friends, stopped going out, stopped working. I concocted ways to avoid seeing certain people until I could starve myself down to even a few pounds lighter. I live in terror of photos people post on the internet of me playing drums. The embarrassment is overwhelming. I swallow this humiliation with every bite of anything.

What is it like to eat? It is mindless, or it is shameful. There is great joy in flavor, in the peace of eating with my family and people I trust, in the celebrations that include a celebration of food. There is an inability to notice when I am full. An inability to stop eating until everything is gone. An insatiable appetite. My father bet his friend once that I could eat more pizza than the friend's son. My aunt told me I could have pancakes if I finished some other food, which I did, and for the first time I felt the horror of someone noticing this ability in me. Always able to eat more food than anyone. Always able to, but why do it? Habit, a pattern, a comfort, a compulsion.

This constant obsession. I could be working on things benefiting the people around me. Or me, for that matter. Writing, creating music, drumming, creating laughter and love and art. Always thinking I'm not good enough to do any of that until I am the correct weight.

What is the frequency of a body without shame? What is the frequency of a reality lived in a creative space without always returning to the misery of the physical form? Why, if I believe we are creating our own reality every second, do I believe there is no escape from this contraction of consciousness?

The clouds clear for a split second, and I see blue sky, the blue, clear, cloudless sky of living in creative spirit with none of the corporeal heaviness and gray shame that holds me earthbound and unable to create. What is the frequency of blue? May I vibrate there?

The body doesn't vibrate except when in meditation, after days and days of examining every little pore of the body and opening them up and letting a free flow of awareness though the pores and membranes of the physical self. Then, on the seventh day, the vibration happens. The frequency of that is the same frequency of the blue. There is joy in spirit and the ability to create and do.

The clouds part and I am in blue sky, a little window of blue sky where the mind and spirit soar. What calls me back is thinking of being onstage. *How did she get so fat?* The inability to work well because I am too heavy. The inability to wear what I am supposed to wear because I am too heavy. The admission of age and time. It all comes rushing in again.

I wonder if Patti went through these issues when getting back to performing again for the first time in fifteen years, if she wondered if people would accept her physical form. Somehow, I don't think so. I see her as living in appreciation of the fact that the people who loved her had loved her well. That she had loved well.

I see myself through the Old Man's eyes and how a younger, sunnier person would be better for him. If I were him, would I want this heavy, still woman around who seems checked out a lot of the time? I am not checked out, just deep in these thoughts, this endless back-and-forth.

I think what he would like most is for me to be happy and joyful. I think that's why he loved me, because I could be fun and silly and joyful and happy. He has a need to play at squashing that down, at not letting it get too happy or silly. He likes the role of the old man raining on parades but secretly loves the parade. It delights me, and I feel sad for what he has signed up for.

Once, in New York, someone anonymously sent me a listing cut from a magazine for a diet aid. It was so hurtful, and helpful as well. I ended up finding a pseudo-doctor and taking diet pills that threatened to give me a heart attack and probably shortened my life in the long run.

I think my boyfriend of the time was behind the letter. The funny thing was, the weight loss and the drugs triggered a manic phase that ended in me leaving him forever. The battle in which I was caught scattered shrapnel across all involved.

The body needs lubrication. The body needs the joy of movement and speed. The body needs still focus with the mind sweeping through it attentively. The body needs fuel. The body needs love when observed in a mirror, love for the strength and soft curves and power. The body needs to be loved and tended and finally made peace with. We can vibrate in that clear blue sky together, shame clouds parting and breathing in the air of creativity and love for manifestation.

What if, in loving my body, I am in love with decorating it, dressing it, making it up, celebrating it? What if I revel in it? There will come a time when I won't be able to use it the way I can now. Why not use it? Why not love its strength and glorious power? Why not care for the skin and the nails, luxuriate in the length of limb, the stretch of tendon, the weight of muscle? Why not love it without judgment?

Why not vibrate in that blue sky where every moment the creative spark is animating this body and its abilities, a true gorgeous creation beyond mind and thoughts and expectations and judgments and history and stories and words. The body is usefulness. The body is joyfulness. The body is as divine as anything else.

The body is an instrument through which we know the divine, the tool we may use to once and for all come into pure presence, pure experience. The physical form is a field on which all manifestation of our struggle to align with the love of the divine is played. It is a great gift of embodiment to have this body through which we enact our desperate attempts to escape and the battle with what is.

I fall into the infinity of sweet air and the joy of typing and of language that comes from the interior and has no need to hide anything. This is all creation from the earth. The gorgeous earth, loamy and dark, births molecules and cells and blood and fibers and hair and skin, just the way it creates lungs disguised as trees and hearts disguised as mollusks and the fingers of the tide tickling the sand with each breath I breathe. I am being breathed, and I am the breather. In the blue ether the air is so pure it fills the pores, then passes through, keeps me floating, keeps the body floating in creation.

I have the blue vibration available to me at any time. The familiar patterns of mind and the contractions of consciousness break apart when I want them to, when I allow them to. This battle of physical form has been as crucial as any other part of me in driving to the understanding of who Clem is beneath it all.

The fear and the shame, they are primarily afraid for themselves. They have created a need for themselves, a necessity that blocks my forward creative movement, creativity in the way I live, creativity in the way I love, creativity of joyfulness and playfulness and fun. Fear and shame did their job of making sure I was safe. I am safe now. They can go.

Beautiful body, go out and experience this blushing sky and the ocean air, warmer at this time of the morning than almost any other part of the day. Beautiful being, open your pores and let in the light and the sound and the smells of the reality you are creating. Beautiful skin, strong legs, powerful core, muscle and sinew and joints and blood, work to create an experience of morning. All of this struggle is nothing but stones on a path to the moment when the gray clouds part and the sun shines into the endlessly blue vibration of true love of being.

Ah, orange-now sky, paling yellow clouds, gray and blues lifting into the dream of a day, the dream of life. Fingers, I love you for these words.

The night before a recording session, I dreamed I was looking in the mirror, a close-up of very crooked snaggleteeth. The dream interpretation book says this is a dream of insecurity, of not feeling good enough. I didn't think I was feeling uncertain of my ability before the recording, but somewhere in subconscious Clem those feelings were probably lurking.

Catching glimpses of news stories as I start my mornings, I wonder how we can ever feel good enough. There seems to be so much evidence to the contrary. Never pretty enough or smart enough, accomplished enough or loved enough. Thin enough, rich enough, healthy enough, young enough . . . the things we need to change seem infinite.

The list is insistent. I haven't been making the right choices. I haven't been the absolute best I can possibly be. The mistakes of my past that landed me here spool out like an endless grocery list. Never enough.

There is horizon out the window, the yellow and gray landscape of western Omaha. The sky rests heavy and seals the earth shut. In my reverie I play with perspective. I see the tableau as a flat backdrop, and I imagine pulling a zipper up through the middle of it, revealing a dark, starlit sky beneath.

I dreamed I was in a room, like an office, and the walls were flimsy and weak. I went over and began shaking the pillars holding up the roof, and as the thin acoustic panels fell around me, I was overwhelmed with the view of the night sky crammed with billions of bright colored stars, every color of star above me and of me. I was breathless with the revelation that I had been falsely under the impression that stars were one color. I fell into the expanse of light. I was under the sky. I was the sky.

How is it possible to be not enough?

The pine trees outside wave at me through the glass. I hear their song wander through the quiet bedroom, a rising chorus of wind and tree. The song exists for me to hear. The sky seals the horizon because I dream it that way. My breath floats through my lungs and through my skin. I am a wisp of smoke in time and space, a collection of particles, a contraction of consciousness. A star and expanse of star.

In a true dream of awareness, we are enough. We are everything. Let me live from this sanctuary. I am see-through, a light that flickers in a millisecond flash. When I shine alongside the other lights in my life, the light of the ones I walk with, the light of those I have known and those I have yet to know, what can be dreamed that is beyond limitation?

At a loss, I made it a point to buckle down to play more drums. Maybe I'm not creating anything of use or inspiration for the world, but I do need to keep my chops up. I wanted to get lost in a place without words, a place of geometry and algebra and primal communication beyond story. What lets loose in the moments of freely beating the drums is ancient language, connected to all time and all language. Drums are the signal to gather, the calling forth of spirit, the connection to a past so long only our cells remember. Drums are magic. I got lost in the magic for a while. I consoled myself with rhythm.

There is a section in one of the songs I can't play smoothly. I slow down the part and play it over and over, like a meditation. Like meditation, I try to be compassionate with myself as I flail through the fills at half-time speed. I have to stop and really spell out each hit, note by note. Then very slowly, I manage it a little faster. The progress is slow but gratifying. There is progress. In that I marvel. I had forgotten what forward movement felt like.

The math of the drums carries me in a cage of comfort. The fill starts with the left hand, then a triplet next to the eighth note run scattered through the toms. I work to break the chains tying the limbs together, those ropes of habit preventing certain patterns. I learn to let go of frustration.

After all of that, I just play. The edges of myself blow away in the eye of the song. My limbs build the mathematical structure in which I drift.

Where is time in this place? Only the song keeps track, and when there is no song and only drums, time breathes deeply across an infinite plane, from so far back it is wordless. I ruminate endlessly on time and space, our souls and where they have traveled. Is it only the human mind registering the forward and back construct? When I play now, does it echo across the years to the place where drums first spoke? Am I merely contributing my voice to a song started long ago?

Or do I play drums in a tribute band, eking out a living by providing a night of escape and romantic trips to memories of golden days. This too. Maybe one day, some writing will come and strike beauty in the world. Maybe one day, a song I play will move someone to hope. Maybe one day, I will find the voice that will inspire change and love and a new way of being in the world, a match sparking compassion like wildfire through humanity.

We are here to witness, to interpret, to be uplifted, and to learn. Poem by poem, song by song, we contribute to the long conversation that started with a first word, spilling from forgotten lips, breaking the silence of eons.

39 A two-night run is wonderful for a musician. The second night feels luxurious. You arrive at the venue and the technicians and stage manager feel like old friends. Your equipment is all set up and waiting for you, like a car prewarmed on a freezing day.

The show started. My body felt strong and capable. I had a warm feeling from the sold-out show the night before. The songs were settled and pocketed.

Then, something happened to call my mind to the stage. Maybe there was some unsteadiness in the band, or maybe some equipment bite, as it often goes when you're slamming wood on metal and fingers get in the way. Suddenly, I began questioning everything. I entered drum fills and at the last minute was unsure which hand to start with. I produced a few measures that sounded as if I was playing the wrong song.

One pattern in particular decided to leave my repertoire for the rest of the set: the triplet roll around the drums. This flourish ends songs and accounts for my favorite shining moments onstage. For the life of me, I could not get them right. The first one failed, and then the next one, and then a fear crept in and interfered with the next one, and then shame spilled out and prevented the next one, and for about seventy-five minutes it became agony and terrible drumming. I was getting more and more distraught, more embarrassed, and all the emotion spilled out on the drums, preventing any finesse.

There was a famous drummer in the audience. I was transported into his head. What I started thinking was, this great accomplished drummer is hearing every mis-stick. He is noticing it all, all the flubs and uneven rolls and very amateurish errors. The more I made mistakes and put myself in his ears, judging it all from afar, the worse I played.

The superstar drummer is a generous and joyful player. I didn't have any reason to worry about his opinion of me, or to think there was any competition in any way between us, as he is a superior player. His presence was just something for my mind to grab on to. My ego wants to rule me, wants to find ways to keep me in this reality, fearful and unsettled, and this night, it found the hook that kept me gasping in poisoned air.

I got offstage and immediately wanted to crawl under a rock.

Musician etiquette dictates that however terrible you feel about how you played, you never let on that you were unhappy with your performance. Doing so negates the happy experience of the person who is complimenting you, so you smile and try to pretend everything was cool.

It felt impossible to pretend, so I smiled and ran away, busied myself with breaking down the drums and the other end-of-show duties. The other drummer was gracious and having a good time. I have had humiliating shows like this in the long past of my career, so I didn't let it ruin anyone's night but my own. Defeat settled in the upper part of my mind and waved at me. I knew we would meet soon.

Sure enough, in the morning, there it was. The heavy feeling made me want to never get out of bed again. The grand excuses for why the bad show happened and incessant conversations took place in my head. I imagined what I would say to anyone who would tell me what they really thought of my playing. I took flights of fantasy and gave up drumming altogether, gave up the band, moved to Minnesota, and became, I don't know, some other person who has nothing to do with drums ever again. (My escape fantasies always involve baking bread.)

I indulged it all for a little while, but I noticed things had changed. The embarrassment was not so crippling, the negative tirades not so sustaining. I felt drawn to go to work.

I sat in meditation and invited in the heavy feeling to fully experience it. It didn't stay long. I dropped through it, into the still, open plane where all ability exists. What I wanted to do was get to the studio and start smoothing out those troublesome patterns. I wanted to get to the drums. This desire split apart my feelings of unworthiness. I fell down, and once again, I am going to get back up. The drums forgive it all once I get back to them and give them the respect and attention they require.

The negative feelings of the night became the fuel I used to get myself to the studio and woodshed for hours. On the second day, a light bulb came on about a song I thought I would never be able to play, and I spent the next week making progress I never expected to make so quickly. I thank humiliation for the instruction.

40 Often, at the end of the night as I'm packing them up, loading them out, someone comments on the extra work of a drummer, all those pieces and the hassle. My standard response is, "That's the price you pay for playing the best instrument."

The constant tactile experience of playing guitar, so much contact with wood and strings, must be comforting. It is different with the drum set. With my kit, the relation is mostly stick onto drumhead.

Still, my drums are alive to me. They have a personality. Workhorses, they are not concerned with any aesthetic concerns or frilliness. They require power and stamina to make them sing out, and they don't suffer a light touch. They just want to be onstage. They are masters at catching the resonant frequencies of the other instruments in the band and ringing out a deeply connected tone. My drums stand up well to the constant traveling; their three-ply shells are light to carry and make their voice particularly loud.

They are my drums, and they sing for me only. I see them from across the room and still feel the way I did the first time I saw them, stacked up in my practice room by a fellow drummer who was planning on selling them. My whole body reached out, and I had a single clear thought: *Oh! There are my drums!*

There is a kind of magic that happens to instruments with so much intense physical connection with their players, and for instruments that are carried close to the body, it must be especially so.

Our energy, our emotions, our vibrations—it is all manifested energetically. Wood is porous, alive. The work and concentration and passion and creativity flowing from hands on a guitar fretboard must sink in and find the soul of the instrument absorbing the energy of the player. I imagine that the feel is second nature, that a player can know the smallest things about the instrument only she would know, learned in hours and hours of such careful and pinpointed touch. The small anomalies, the rise of the frets, the weight of the strings and their distance to the neck. The little things only the fingers recognize.

So much emotion is transmitted into an instrument, so many moments of pure focus, of attention, of breakthroughs and live energy. So many times reached for to comfort, to console, to soothe. Cried over, danced with, dreamed upon. Every aspiration and fantasy, every night of slogging it out or frustration or sold-out show is lived with the instrument in hand, the instrument an extension of the body, the player's heart manifested on the outside.

I have developed a list of stereotypes about the different players in a band. Of course, stereotypes are limits, and there are always exceptions, but I have fun thinking about it. Certain personality types are drawn to the different instruments, and I have seen enough of a pattern to believe it.

Drummers are often the planners, the organizers, the energy, the drivers. They are often very dorky, those science-fiction-loving, uncool folks who let their freak flags fly with not a lot of concern as to how hip they are perceived to be. I am including myself in this. (Two words: fanny pack.)

Lead guitarists tend to be meticulous, exacting, humble, and insecure in the sense that they rarely believe they are as good as they are.

Rhythm guitarists: sex incarnate.

Singers are wild cards, with simmering unrest at their base. That unrest can either make for someone for whom you are driven to want to do everything, or someone from whom you are driven to get away.

Pianists are mathematicians, colored with streaks of perversion.

Bassists—they may be my favorite. Deep, private, with their own secret garden never revealed. They are usually wonderful company. Funny, wry, easygoing, smart. They do not need to be the center of the party, but the party pulls toward them. Strange and interesting in their ways, they tend to disappear and reappear, with a kind of magic intuition as to when they're needed.

There is something about those low and long sound waves that translate into an intuitive spookiness I have witnessed in bass players I have as friends. They are often slow to react but incredibly thoughtful and prescient when they do.

42 "Healthy competition," team sports, militarism: I have so little ability to align myself to these things. We see stags fighting for the right to mate, extrapolate this as competition in nature, and draw the conclusion we are so ingrained.

The dismantling of beliefs is a fascination of mine. What have I refused to question? It seems by uncovering assumptions, our healing begins.

I embrace the natural joyousness of play and the good-hearted nature of a game. I like to win at games, and in meditation I see a part of my ego that needs to be special or first. I don't take pride in that tendency. I see it as a contorted reflection of my feeling that I am ultimately unlovable.

I reject the idea that without the drive to competition, the duel to the death, we are not human. Competition is a result of a belief in limited resources. We learn something from the bonobo apes:

> "The egalitarian and peaceful bonobo society might have evolved as a result of reduced competition due to the abundance of food in their habitats."[9]

We are born to cooperate, to develop our natural empathy, and as the frontal cortex develops, we progress from the infant's self-centeredness to developing a desire for everyone to thrive. Our first experience in life is the receipt of compassionate care, the mother offering her breast for sustenance.

When we begin believing there is not enough for everyone, humanity buys into the idea that competition is what makes the world go round. Of course, there are those who understand this and create the circumstances reinforcing this perception through their greed.

We are trained to bring competition into the music world as well. The belief is that everyone is out for themselves, and our success means failure for everyone else. We think there is only one way, only one paradigm of success, a limited resource. If we are not the Beatles or the Rolling Stones, or look just like them, emulate their path, then we will give up, as they are the standard for rock-and-roll bands. If we never step off an airplane to throngs of young women screaming our names, we have failed.

We watch competitions of musicians, battles of the bands, "drum-offs." Society loves to pit us against each other. Then, if we haven't beaten down all other drummers and emerged the victor of all the spoils by a particular age, then age becomes the competition, and we are pitted against time.

We hardly ever question these beliefs. Most nights, when I get offstage, someone wants me to know they like me better than another drummer, or another female drummer, or even sometimes my bandmates. I say this lightly, as I overhear my bandmates getting told the same thing about themselves.

The musicians I respect know there is no use for these feelings and that if you are forever looking for validation based on what is happening for everyone around you, your joy in playing music diminishes. These patterns, though, are learned young. Even the most enlightened among us can have moments in which they see someone achieve something musically and feel a sense of failure and envy wash over them.

One way around these feelings is to believe that if the people you associate with achieve success, you are elevated by the association. It is the measure of success that is the issue, and we get to define that for ourselves. There are myriad ways to define success. Each musician gets to find their own.

I have a secret weapon against this struggle. It is something I use whenever I have any sort of issue with a person: envy, frustration, anger, fear. I use it for people I know and for people I don't know. A fellow musician, a jerky neighbor, political figures.

First, I drop into my heart, beneath my thoughts and emotions.

I ask myself, *Who is being injured?* I answer, *Clem is being injured*, and I list the ways.

I ask myself, *What part of Clem is injured?* I find the aspect that feels attached to the injury: the crying child, the embarrassed teen, the drummer ego, the one who believes she is not enough and is terrified everyone can see it. The one who has defined her success by some external standard that is not her own.

I ask, *Where is the part not injured?*

I sit for a while in space and stillness. I breathe deeply. I ask myself, *Who am I?*

Beneath Clementine, I find the energy below, no harm visible.

Then, I bring up the image of the person who is of issue. I see them in front of me, and when I look at them from this place, I nearly always immediately see vulnerability. Each personality is vulnerable. Every human has a soft center. If I can't see it because my vision is obscured by my feelings of envy or frustration, I reduce the person to their child self, see them as their pre-problem self. The power I give to them diminishes. Now, they are just a person, like me, moving through life the best they can.

When I discover this vulnerability, I know because my heart opens. I feel our connection. I feel the desire for them to find their way to light, to success that serves their highest purpose. I recognize that should they reach this elevation, it only serves to elevate me as well.

I open, and a wave of compassion sweeps through me. I set the image of the person spinning, and I bathe them in loving-kindness.

Maybe they won't change at all, so bathed. But now, I have changed my relationship to them. I have changed the power I give them to affect my life. Now, I want only what is best for them. Now, I celebrate their success and feel happy to see we are each on our own path, validating the other by our common goals.

I love to say I have figured out the lazy musician's road to success: align yourself with musicians who work diligently and impeccably and achieve great notoriety and success, and by association your lazy butt gets to reap the rewards. Of course, I must earn the right to play with these folks, so the whole thing falls apart when I look too closely at the joke, but it is true when I say I desire my comrades to achieve all the success of their dreams. They thus elevate the field on which I play.

There was a great gift in starting to play drums so long after most of my fellow musicians had been playing. For many years, I knew that any drummer I shared the stage with was a far superior player than me. This was a relief beyond relief. I didn't have anything to prove. How could I top someone who had started playing at thirteen years old with their buddies in their parents' garage?

When I started playing, I would ask musicians if they wanted to get together and jam, and the inquiry was met with puzzled looks. These were professional musicians by this point. They didn't "jam out" anymore. They had done that through their teen years. I quickly learned I was on my own to develop my playing.

When I got onstage, all I had to do was my own thing. I was never going to be "better" than another drummer. All I could do was what I could do and celebrate what they did too.

The freedom of that was immense. Without a sense of competing with anyone but myself, I got to develop my own voice outside of the idea there were limited spots for those who were stepping up. Maybe if I had started playing at thirteen years old, my life would have fed on competition to get to the top. Instead, my life as a musician has been about being grateful every time I was allowed on the stage. I get to do this? It's all gravy.

I guess the solution to humanity's suffering is to realize there is enough for everyone. The belief that we are to spend our lives scrabbling for more, this scarcity mentality, is perpetuated on every level. We think we are not enough.

This external reach for hoarding, keeping things to ourselves, believing if someone has something we must have more—it is all suffering. We will continue to feel this way until we understand we are indeed deeply loveable, and loved. When we look around and see we have everything we could ever need, our natural generosity rises. Sharing our gifts with others becomes the purpose and delight of life.

43 The band was putting out videos of music lessons. I added meditation videos and a couple of new music videos.

With all this video-making, I realized that my skin has grown thicker. With the all the internal examination and the loosening of ego attachments in a million small ways, the injuries that would have once set me into a tailspin have let go of their sting.

In light of this, I volunteered to be the enforcer, the one who reads through the YouTube comments to approve or delete.

When it comes to social media, negativity is like a drop of blood in the water signaling frenzy, and we have all seen how it rapidly expands and foments and devolves. In the band's first music video, we had no one to monitor the comments. We allowed them through and left them unchecked. I never saw any of them, for all these years. The idea of having to absorb all the negative stuff kept me away. I could only imagine the awfulness there and avoided reading any of it.

At the beginning of the internet, it seemed humanity was surprised to see this tendency spelled out so graphically. Is that what we do? We build up and praise for a while until one person voices a negative thought, and then we indulge the backslide? Here it was, all mapped out: the one-upmanship of insult, the tantalizing opportunity to abase, and above all, the seemingly gleeful nature of the infliction of hurt.

I have recognized this tendency in myself. I am aware of the energizing sensations of the indulgence of gossip, the intoxication of negativity. A negative comment can snowball and become a complete teardown of the offender's character, and the connection with fellow bashers can be like a sick comfort.

When I hear myself succumb to such conversation, I am also aware of the heaviness, the way my balance is upset, and the lower frequency and vibration in which I move. The more I notice how I feel, the more it physically hurts to indulge so.

Damn it. Once again, mindfulness takes all the fun out of stuff.

It occurred to me I didn't think there was anything anyone could say about my drumming or my physical form or my knowledge or my personality or my being worse than what I have said about myself over and over and over since I was about eleven.

That relentless megaphone of negativity has shut the hell up most days, after all these years of working to let it go. I thought it might be an interesting experiment to see what people had said on the videos, which comments triggered my attachment to ego and the places where I am still stuck and feel the hurt of injury. I volunteered to take the foray into the world of YouTube comments.

The women in the band understand that when you create something and put it out for the public, negativity comes with the territory. You have to just let it go. However, when it came to the educational videos, there was a consensus. All the content we were creating was done from a feeling of wanting to share what we had learned playing music we love dearly. We would probably be out of pocket financially for a very long time for each video due to the value of hours of time spent researching and writing and recording and editing. Our consensus was that we would nip any negative comments in the bud. If people chose to exercise their wit and critical skills on the music videos, okay, but on the lessons, we figured the injurious could go elsewhere. This meant someone needed to monitor the comments.

My first stop was on our first video from 2010, the one with eighteen million views and over twenty thousand comments. I thought to peruse these first, to see if I really had crossed the line beyond giving a crap about what people said.

The first wonderful thing was that I had no idea how little negativity there was, at least in the four hundred or so comments I scrolled through. Some people didn't like the performance for various reasons. Okay, their prerogative. I was not sure how on earth a human could have time to search out something they didn't like and then spend time commenting, but whatever. It didn't bug me if they felt like voicing an opinion.

There was a lot of sexual stuff, which was predictable given that the band is made up of women. As a culture we have a way to go, obviously. It was as I expected. As long as it wasn't threatening or graphic, I let the comment live. Predictable. Antiquated. By leaving that stuff on there, I hoped eventually these folks would be schooled on basic etiquette by others, which they were. My heart leaped at the rational and kind correctors.

There were a couple of statements that were so overtly sexist I laughed out loud, taking it as a joke. My favorite—"Who is making the sandwiches while all this malarkey is going on?"—still cracks me up. This kind of sexism is so silly I find it funny. I grew up in a liberal family where the off-color joke was celebrated, and I laugh because the idea of someone actually thinking this way is so ludicrous.

White-supremacist and cultish religiosity—there were maybe a handful of those comments, cries for attention I deleted. Mansplaining about the sound or techniques: expected and usually incorrect. Some good critiques. I left all of those. In fact, I only deleted a handful of those things that made me cringe to read and which seemed to be there for the most injury and shock value and divisiveness. This doesn't mean I necessarily liked everything I read, but I also saw the whole forum as something unto itself, that I policed lightly and didn't take personally at all.

I felt pretty good and kind of amazed at how far I had come and overwhelmed by the kindness shown to the band. I realized that in avoiding the negative, I had missed out on the positive. I felt guilty for letting my fragility take over, for all the ways I had decided to believe that humans were predominately not wonderful.

When we posted the new music videos and the educational videos, I felt happy to be the comment reviewer. I was again overwhelmed with the kindness shown to the band. I basked in gratitude, even when people cared enough to say they didn't like it.

Then, the big test came when someone commented that I had gained weight in the eight years since the previous video. For most of my life I would have not been able to handle such an observation. It was almost a relief to see my worst-case scenario spelled out: someone calling me fat.

My first thought was, *Duh, I'm the one who had to buy new pants.* I deleted it and went on with my day.

It was then I knew that whatever attachments have been torturing me have loosened. Yes, body changes, weight gains and losses, okay. I reflected on how much of my life has been spent in the analysis of my physical form, a gripping tension, an agony of control. Sometimes I remind myself that one day I may be very thin, wasted away by illness, or old age if I am very lucky. I anticipate that then, my whole life of dieting will pass before me with regret.

When I was thin, I thought I was fat. Now I work to be healthy, all of it in a public eye that spends 90 percent of the time saying ridiculously kind things to me about the way I play drums and the things I create and say.

I don't care, anymore. Goodbye, old life. Goodbye, hating myself at every incarnation. Hello, self-compassion. Hello, my dear heart so capable of love for humanity. Hello, delete button.

I was feeling pretty good about it all. Then, there was a comment on one of the meditation videos I created as a bonus to the educational channel: "I don't think you should break the fourth wall with your fans."

This was interesting to me. I understand the sentiment. I know what it is like to fall in love with a persona only to discover a totally different one offstage. There is a singer I know who is so incredibly sexy onstage, then offstage I find her uptight, self-absorbed, and boring. I have encountered this many times.

The first widely known artist I knew personally was in New York City. We sat at a bar, having a conversation about philosophy and books. Interrupting this rapt bubble of connection was a nice person who came over to effuse to the artist about his work. I was amazed to see a mask shut the artist's face like a steel door, this man who had been so open, so connected, so free just moments before. With a compliment, all the light went out and the mask came down. He repeated gratitude platitudes over and over until the person left. Then, the door stayed shut, and we couldn't return to the conversation. It was as if he forgot he was able to let the door open at all.

I began to question myself. Should I not share the meditations and the blog and the videos? Does knowing I meditate before the shows, or that I am thoughtful about a number of esoteric things, or that I am a pretty nerdy goofball, or that I write these words—does this ruin the show for people paying to see me play drums?

In the last educational video I filmed, I became overcome talking about how grateful I am to share my art with others, and I started to cry mid-video. This was hysterically funny to my bandmates, and to me. "Did you just make yourself cry?"

My first instinct was to cut this blubbering out of the video, but then I thought, why on earth am I ashamed of being moved by connection? Why is it that expressing real feeling can be so mortifying?

Onstage, I aim to be huge. Powerful. Ecstatic. Does all this other stuff negate that? Does the power seem put-on if my power lies in stillness?

I started to read into that YouTube comment. Are they saying they like their version of me more than the reality of me? Well, in that case, I am sunk. Because I can't possibly be any different from what I am. In fact, if the commenter were to really look at it from an esoteric perspective, the vision of me they are seeing is only a reflection of their own history and DNA and preferences and creations. If I offend their desire for me to be a certain way, then who is doing the offending?

I will never understand how to be a public figure any more than I understand how to be a private figure. I am alternately aloof and too open, truthful and non-disclosing, grumpy and effusive. In short, the glorious dichotomy of a human. What would it be like for us to see the other not through our filter but as another being connected right through the heart? You are me, and I am you. All the unpleasant parts of you are me. Maybe what I detest in others is what I hate most in myself but am not willing to see.

I want to say that opening oneself to be vulnerable feels like flying. First you must push yourself out of the plane, out the open door through the barrier of fear: fat and sappy and dumb and weak. But once you get over the ledge, once you think: You know what? Hanging out in this loud, annoying, metal contraption of a mind is over for me. I can't take it anymore! Then, you realize there is no plane. When we can't take it anymore and we throw ourselves overboard into the vast sky of the heart, I have to tell you, it is truly like flying. And once you're out, you really can't get back in the same way.

Once you read every single comment, once you see how much beauty there is and how little cruelty, once you realize how each negative comment is either a legitimate dislike or a legitimate cry for attention, once you realize that you are *done* with listening to the megaphone of negativity pumping through your brain to keep you afraid of writing or of playing or of loving, then you are flying, man. You are flying.

In Duncan Trussell's podcast,[10] he related a story of attending a Ram Dass retreat on Maui. During a kirtan, when there was divine music being played and everyone was dancing, someone asked him to dance. He replied: "Not in this incarnation."

As the rest of the party happened around him, he zoomed his awareness up and saw himself sitting there, trapped in a box of rules he had constructed for himself: *I guess in this lifetime, I don't dance during a kirtan.* He could see the little part of himself that really *did* want to dance, trapped there, in a big metal cage of his own making. He realized he didn't want to be in a cage anymore.

What I fear shines the light on what it is time to let go of. I leap out of my cage of fear into love. I love it all. I love you all, no matter what you say.

THE LEMON SONG

44 "The Lemon Song" is our sound check song, the warm-up song. Guitar enters first, and tone takes control of the room, establishes the main voice. Then comes crashing the groove. The electrifying vocal. The dynamic range. The tasty raunch. The fun little fills. The ascension of the solo section, a free-for-all which froths up an energy in the room that is the reason audiences like bands who play this music. If you did see Zeppelin, you saw them at a festival or in a stadium or auditorium. You didn't see them in a small rock club. The tangible freneticism of those solo sections overtakes a room and everyone in it. This is what you got all dolled up for.

Parts like this have gotten my band into trouble with the sound police. It is not so much that we are a particularly loud band, but when we focus on creating energetic volume, you will be a little bowled over, and promoters get scared. I have walked through venues before a show introducing myself and handing out earplugs so the promoter didn't have a heart attack. Some promoters don't realize that volume and energy is why people come to listen to Led Zeppelin's music. The audience is with us from the get-go.

"The Lemon Song" is just fun to play. The fills are to the drummer as play is to an otter. They are within reasonable technical ability, but they are also interesting, delicious little patterns that are unusual, and thus memorable.

We carry on multiple conversations in the background throughout the song. The vocal and drum conversation is particularly fun, as it is responding to a conversation the vocal and the guitar are having. The drums are the friend standing back, listening to two friends figure something out. The drummer and bassist have their own dance happening while they listen intently to what's happening over there.

I regret ways I have behaved in band relationships. It can be splendid and difficult to work so closely with others, when friendship and creative choice and business all mingle. This aspect of my life has engendered in me a kind of clarity and honesty in communication that is a bit intense to people.

Gretchen and I have worked together for many years. Other than random snippy moments in the ocean of fatigue and travel, we have had no major dustups. That is remarkable and says more about her ability to communicate than anything. With others and in other moments, I have been reactive. A band leader must be clear with boundaries, and many are not. I have struggled with them. I tend to want to do too much, and then when I set a boundary it is much too late. All previous kindness becomes suspect. Bad feelings develop and last.

Female bands are magical and difficult, since the intuitive abilities of women, and creative women, can lead to psychological assumptions and hurts so subtle they cause resentments we may never uncover. We know so much about the struggles we each carry, discussed and analyzed for mile after mile as we drive. This makes it easy to avoid conflict, but once conflict happens, it can be profoundly unsettling to have gotten so close and bared so much. The ammunition for attack is laid out. Will we go there? Fisticuffs or knives?

I was breaking up with a man I had been dating. He was in another city, and I was on the phone for three days: *It's not you, it's me.* Trying to let him down easy, to let him know that what we had shared was valuable to me but now had no future.

I was in the recording studio and kept getting called away for these conversations. I needed to focus, yet my desire to not cause this person pain kept me distracted.

Finally, I was tired. I needed my attention back. I needed for him to hear me. I blurted out: *Listen. It's over. I am not in love with you. I fell in love with someone else.*

He said, *Thank you, Clementine.* And hung up.

This was a lesson in short, sweet, to the point. Rip the Band-Aid off. By being clear in my language and intent, I show respect for the other person's ability to handle difficult information. It keeps each person in their power. No one likes being shielded and babied.

I have tried my best to approach conversation this way in bands, speaking kindly and directly, but I get wrapped up in trying to make people happy.

As a child, when I would have a party and a friend would feel sick, as would happen at most children's parties, I would breathe deeply, try to will their sickness into me. I knew if I were sick, I would still be able to have fun. I didn't want anyone to miss out.

I learned later that this is a misinformed *tonglen* practice, a Buddhist technique of relieving the suffering of others. In tonglen, we are not to bring the pain into ourselves and take it on or hold it. We learn to allow it to move through and release.

I have learned if I try to take on the other person's suffering, I disempower them. Each person must take responsibility for speaking their feelings and for holding the response. For too long I believed I was responsible for everyone's pain and in this caused so much more pain.

Certainly, I am not saying I behaved as Mother Teresa in moments of ending. I lashed out, was unkind, and out of frustration held on to battles that would have been better to let go.

There are people in the world who will never forgive my decisions to set boundaries, to end things. Either I perceived we had each moved on, whether they could see it or not, or something broke beyond repair. I regret my inability to handle endings well. I can only hope what I have learned continues forward.

I consider each person and situation I encounter as a teacher. This seems easy to do with someone we care for or feel sorry for—lesson in love, lesson in compassion—but harder when who or what we encounter is challenging. The driver cuts me off and my first instinct is not to thank him for teaching me patience or forgiveness. I don't immediately recognize gratitude for his lesson in nonreactivity. I really want to flip him the bird, and sometimes, I do.

The person with whom we can't find resolution seems nothing but a painful frustration. We feel misery and suffering for the experience, not gratitude for the lesson.

All the difficulties I have had with people show me my own inabilities to communicate, to understand, to empathize. The person offends me by saying something I just can't forgive, and I endure a contraction of anger. A spotlight shines on the limits of my compassion, my limited ability to rise above ego slights to find a way to resolution. The ego collapses and withdraws or lashes out. The suffering that rises is the understanding that self-realization is further away than I fool myself into believing.

Here, then, is a teacher showing me the progress I am still to make. Can I bring myself to feel gratitude for the lesson? This can seem impossible. If we give someone credit for the teaching moment, we feel we are giving up our rights, our feeling of self-worth, our self-esteem. If we give even an inch, if we acknowledge there may be something in us that needs addressing, some failing that needs to be understood, then we're a pushover, a doormat. If we don't stand our ground, we are worse than incapable. Ineffectual.

We hold on to our opinions and defenses, and we grip our sense of righteousness so tightly we become stone. We define our sense of self by the injury and the ability to battle such an attack. We fight to withstand slings and arrows. We know ourselves as forthright and decisive and pillars of strength and, meanwhile, dig ourselves into more misery.

When do we forget we spin here, together, as one vibration thrumming infinity?

46

Monday morning at the day job. The band drove eleven hours from a show in Portland the day before, and since the club sold out, we got a late start on Sunday morning. After-party at a friend's house. Drinks by the backyard firepit. Laughing so hard it hurt.

The stale law firm air hits me in the face like humility. The double life amuses me at this point. Saturday night, I autographed a man's chest after the show. Blink, and I am sitting in a cubicle with my hair in a bun.

I pour water over a teabag as one of the attorneys sidles up. A scarecrow of a man, there is kindness buried in there somewhere, long tamped down by the need to do The Right Thing. He tells me a story about his daughter playing drums at a recital, how much she likes it, how her talent blew him away.

I respond with enthusiasm and try to be as encouraging as possible.

"Does she have a teacher she likes? It's so important for a musician of any age to find a teacher she really connects with. You can buy a drum set for pretty cheap, or practice pads to have in the house for her to do hand exercises on." I ramble on about various ideas to further his daughter's education.

I finish my little speech and look up from my teacup. He is staring at me with uncharacteristic frankness, mouth open. He has made the connection between encouraging his daughter and his Marin County, Ivy League, Do The Right Thing plan for her.

"Yes, but then she might want to be a musician!"

Good breeding and buried kindness telegraph across his face in a flash of regret for his words, but the horror in his voice gives him completely away.

I get it. He probably hopes his daughter ends up a securities lawyer. Huge bank accounts and houses and cars and vacations: the American Dream. The fact I would rather carry a bass guitar cabinet called "The Fridge" for a living makes no difference. My life is definitely not for everyone.

Regardless of the scarecrow's dreams for his daughter's life, without drums she might be shuffling through junior high hallways right now, powerless. Hitting something very hard at that, or any age, is a revelation, a connection to an inner understanding of strength that will always serve her well.

47 Junior high school. Taller than any other student and some of my teachers, I'm walking to a school assembly with shoulders compressed to force my head toward my sternum, eyes on the ground. Due to a limited imagination, a very sporty girl has decided to make me the target of her ridicule as we jostle in the pack heading toward the auditorium. This is Southern California, so the stage is outside, center of the school. The sunlight is blinding enough so when I hear this girl behind me, I am able to do a quick turn to evade her path and slide onto a bench at the back without her seeing.

The high school jazz band is warming up as the quad fills. I watch my tormentor take her seat, and I relax and check the band out. I wish away this school and look to the stage for a sign that high school is different. There are about seven worldly teenagers there, looking bored and fiddling with their instruments. Guitar, saxophone, trumpet, a big upright guitar, a keyboard. My eyes study each one.

At this point, I have played perfunctory piano for about six years. Perfunctory guitar for a summer. Perfunctory flute through elementary school.

There is a girl onstage. I watch her come from the right, say something to the guitar player, smile coolly, and walk to the drums. The drummer is a girl. An electric tingle of surprise squares my shoulders, and I sit up straight. The drummer doesn't call attention to herself. No one onstage makes a big deal or regards her in any special way, yet I watch this foreign entity as I would watch a macaw fluttering down into the Serrano Middle School quad. She sits at the drums, adjusts one of the stands, then reposes there patiently, a part of the ensemble.

The band starts to play, and I watch her confidently drive the music and move effortlessly through the magical patterns she plays on the drums. The band members seem centered around her, and she leads the aggressive sound as it bounces through the stone auditorium. She isn't smiling or trying to ingratiate herself. She is an elegant mix of physical power and beauty. For the entire hour, I am on that stage, in the driver's seat.

I hear nothing but drums in my head for the rest of the day. How do I tell my parents this is now my chosen instrument? I try a variety of scenarios and reasons.

"But you've already played the piano, guitar, and flute, and you never stuck with any of them!"

My parents would never go for yet another instrument. With this realization I am forlorn and shuffle home, head hanging in defeat. The idea of telling my parents I want to learn the drums is just too much.

Funny thing, they probably would have encouraged it. I am grateful for the way things turned out, but I must say I wonder what it would have been like to have been brave then and to have met the call.

48 When I started drumming, it connected with something so deep it was different from anything else, as if I had stumbled on a language that went beyond language, yet one I understood without learning. I have played drumbeats that felt like they were coming through me and were beyond my understanding. Not that they were particularly fancy or difficult, just that they seemed to have a transmission in them that reached very far back and carried an energy far vaster than a rock song on a Saturday night. Little moments, little glimpses into vibrations that manifest and connect. A vibration of spirit, or an echo that took eons to slap back through those big floor toms.

I hope that if someone in the future is coming back to investigate, riding in on some time-traveling apparatus, body-hopping experiences from long ago, I hope they get to feel what I feel when I'm playing the drums. That's the way to get closest to Clem.

49 Summer has always been my least favorite season. For me, it is the gloomy season. This belief has something to do with loving school as a child. Summer meant boredom, missing the social interaction of the classroom and the stimulation of learning. When I put myself back there, I lie in my bedroom feeling the incessant breath of the air conditioner, listening to the mosquito buzz of a lawn mower or a plane whining through the sky. Everyone elsewhere, everyone gone. Humanity splashes gloriously in the warm sunshine as I sit in a prison of tedium.

Many have such stories. Through these experiences we develop patterns of thought and emotion, and we think, this is who I am. I say, I am gloomy when it gets hot out. I say, I tend toward depression in the summer. I attach myself to that concept, that thing I am. I tell the story, and I get depressed. I attach myself to all the stories of my childhood, the feelings of frustration, the loneliness, the disconnection.

Summer is my least favorite season, I say. *In summer, I get depressed.*

This is our pattern of living, the pattern of life. First, I feel an emotion. I tell myself the story of the emotion, review all the reasons for its existence. I berate myself for feeling the emotion. Then, I judge, see myself as weak for feeling this way. Then, I push the emotion away, find a bunch of ways to distract myself from the feeling. Then, I fail to avoid the emotion and lose the battle. Then, it begins all over: dismay, judgment, avoidance, fall. All of this keeps the pattern in place, reinforces it.

It's just how I am, I say.

For instance: I get depressed in summer. I tell myself I feel this way because of experiences in my childhood. I tell this story and feel all the old wrongs. I judge the emotion. I feel ridiculous for disliking everyone's favorite season, and I tell myself I am weak for associating summer with feeling lonely. There must be something wrong with me for being lonely in summer. If I get up every morning and go out for a bike ride, eat mostly fruit and make myself very busy, then maybe I will avoid feeling depressed. This works for a while, until an afternoon comes when the emotion is unavoidable, the depression spreads, and there it is, that feeling again. Now I feel even worse because I tried to avoid it but failed.

From that still place beneath the ego, beneath Clementine, I see the emotions, the thoughts, the concepts, and I no longer react to them. A feeling of loneliness passes through, and I say, *Ah, loneliness. Let me observe it.*

A story rises, and I descend into stillness. When I feel lonely, there is heat behind my eyes. There is a tightness in my chest I associate with sadness. There is sadness, an aching feeling in my torso. Let me invite this in. Let me feel this fully. I sit and feel this gaping pain.

Sometimes it feels as though I might die if I allow myself to feel this emotion. It has never come to that. I can always take the weight, no matter how strong the feeling.

After a while of doing this, keeping myself neutral, observing emotions, detached from the stories I would normally tell, I start to notice that there is a part of myself where sadness doesn't exist. Often, once I allow the emotion in completely, face it and feel it fully, then I am amazed to see how quickly it disperses. What is there instead? Sometimes, another heaviness to release. Sometimes, an opposite emotion: lightness, joy.

To these pleasant emotions, I am neutral as well. Let me observe. Let me sit in this still, peaceful place and let that joy fill me up. The tingly sensation of happiness passes through. This too will change.

I let go of battle and effort. Here, the place of no story, no past or future. Right here.

50

In the early mornings, the house is still, the air fresh and smelling of sea. The salty crispness makes me think of those early morning swimmers at Aquatic Park, the little cove off the San Francisco Bay that is a short walk from my apartment.

The San Francisco Bay is an estuary, which means the ocean washes in and out, and the water is surprisingly clean, at least at Aquatic Park. How bracing it is to step into the water first thing in the morning. Your mind gets wiped clear when you swim in ice water as the sun rises.

Since I moved to San Francisco, I have wanted to believe I have the stuff to make this happen every morning. As of this writing, I do not. The water is so cold I can't catch my breath, even in a wetsuit, even on warm days. Then, I can't stop thinking of sea lions and how years ago there was one who took umbrage to the swimmers and took a few bites. The movie *Jaws* really complicated saltwater swimming for so many of us.

When I have tried to swim here, I made sure to be the closest swimmer to the beach, believing other swimmers to be chum, I guess. That must break one of the Buddhist precepts somehow.

Something about man-made objects in the water freaks me out. Seeing footage of divers coming upon sunken ships sends an electric thrill and queasiness through me, and I can barely watch. The underside of buoys or boats, the still, barnacled legs of piers, even the pavement of a boat launch ramp shivers dread through my body. When returning to shore, I can never touch down until I am in a couple feet of water, terrified of what my toes will encounter. In the Bay, I stay far away from the bend in the cove where all the mossy rocks lie still and sleeping underneath. I could never swim in proximity to the big ships on the right edge. My map of available swimming area in the small cove gets smaller and smaller as I imagine all possible underwater encounters.

How wonderful it must be to relax into a nice long swimmer's stroke, without the need to flip turn, without the claustrophobia or ickiness of the public pool. The regular swimmers in the Bay are marvels. Their even and meditative forms slide through the water with a silver elegance. When I try it, I get into a rhythm and then panic as I drift a little farther out than normal, or I get close to a buoy, or the dark of the water changes, or I encounter one of those pockets of very cold water. Dread tracks through my body. I stop mid-stroke and sort of flail around, gasping, until I find some fortitude and buck up again.

I do love to float on my back and watch the sky. Once or twice, I made it into the water as the sun was rising or setting, and the sky beyond the Golden Gate Bridge was a marvel. Those moments were worth it all. I didn't think about what was underneath. I watched the rose clouds blossom and change, and I allowed that peaceful, floating-on-my-back joy to wash through me.

Eventually though, the thought of those fit folks and their steady paces behind me brought the old shame to the surface. I can't keep up. I am a failure. Or suddenly, my internal vision would drop beneath me, at the bottom looking up. I would see my body on the surface, all space and darkness in between bottom and top. Again, I would flail about with a kind of vertigo, panting. I would berate myself, power through, invent a stroke to mimic the real swimmers out there, finding strength and pushing away the fear for short bursts. Then, the recognition I was kidding myself would dawn on me. I would paddle in defeat to shore.

It is funny to watch myself unable to get over these fears. The thing is, what is it I am really afraid of? The underside of things, the unknown, things being out of order, the unexpected. As someone who sits in meditation and observes all manner of shame and fear tracking through, contorting the body, manifesting as pain, then releasing, you'd think I would be able to get over it and make a regular morning practice of getting in the water. As someone who regularly performs feats of strength, drives for hours, loads equipment, plays drums for two hours through pain and illness, you'd think I would at least be able to power through the uncomfortable aspects of a morning swim.

As a Southern California child, I was in the Pacific Ocean and lakes and swimming pools for hours and hours and hours. I could swim to China. I have endless swimming stamina.

After a short walk, I could step into a relatively clean, relatively safe body of water and spend an hour in the long, slow freestyle I learned as a child. I love the rhythm of the breathing: three strokes on the right, breath, three strokes on the left, breath. I love how long I feel, how weightless. I love all the little adjustments I make as I go and how I let go of thinking about form. My mind sails away into stillness, or into story, and I watch my thoughts as they rise and evaporate. I love the peace. I love the way my body feels as I rise from the water after a swim, shaking yet powerful. I love the exquisite warm shower after.

So why doesn't this practice become a part of my life? The first answer my mind always gives: it is too cold. This is a truth. The water in the Bay is very cold. Even in a wetsuit, my feet, hands, and face go numb. The center of my body clenches so tightly, protecting my organs from the shock, that the pain in my back becomes agonizing. Temperature is the first battle to overcome.

Physical pain is the easiest to avoid. The underwater issues, those are probably the real reason I avoid the experience, but the mind uses the pain of the cold to keep me snug on the couch in the early mornings, instead of experiencing the shock of fifty-four degrees.

My mentor Sirriya's experience of awakening involves cold. She says there was a certain feeling, an energy, she kept feeling over a shoulder. She avoided investigating this feeling because it felt cold, and she associated cold with darkness and fear. It was only when she finally turned into this feeling, really investigated this cold, by sitting and opening to what she would find there, only then did she drop through all the patterns and conditioning holding her back from realizing her infinite self.

The sky is lavender at 6:30 a.m. I imagine getting up, throwing on a sweatsuit over a swimsuit, grabbing the wetsuit, and leaving the pug nestled in bed. I imagine walking down the hill to the beach club, through the morning streets, which in San Francisco are always surprisingly warm and still. It is often the warmest time of the day, I have found, as the ocean breeze quiets. I imagine pulling on the suit and wading into the cold water. I imagine finally committing, starting the stroke and noticing how long it takes for my muscles to let go of the clenching protection, noticing the mind and how soon it quiets, watching as fear tries to take hold and fails. I watch as I make my peace with the underneath, all its mystery and unexpected lessons.

It's a beautiful vision. I feel strong just imagining it.

5 1 I am in the quietest place I know, with only
the sound of fog getting sucked into trees,
the distant crashing of waves on shore, and
an occasional airborne racket: human, bird, or fly. The scut-
tling of lizards through the brush agitates a tiny ripple in the
warm air. I take the day into my lungs and through me, into
this moment. Then this one.

A thin dragonfly sets down alongside the path on my walk
through the trees, and it stops me cold. It is a color of blue un-
imaginable. His big eyes swivel to look at me for a long time.
I swear he looks happily curious. He has a blue band of a flag
at the end of his long body, and I lean down and marvel at it.
For some period of time, all sound is gone. The air is still. The
dragonfly quivers in delight then stills, quivers then stills. We
share the stillness.

It occurs to me to leave. I follow the thought, break the
trance, and take a step before he seems ready to see me go. He
startles me by streaking in front of my eyes, the blue a neon
light trailing across my vision. Surrender To The Now! his
banner waves.

The next morning, I drift down the bright San Francisco
sidewalk with the Old Man and the pug, heading to our favorite diner on Fisherman's Wharf. I remember that a few days
past I had been investigating my internal attachments.

Suddenly, I step out of the river of thought rushing above
me into quiet. My steps ring vibration on the bright white

sidewalk. The cream and pastel buildings reflect a shimmer in the air. The blue sky is dressed in a mosaic of white cloud lace.

It is almost a physical sensation, stepping out of the river, as if stepping out of water perfectly dry. For most of the walk, thoughts blow by above as I walk right in the center of morning.

DAZED AND CONFUSED

52

"Dazed and Confused" is a journey into spaces where the emotion of Bonham's playing is a watercourse carrying us through. There is abandon in the intensity, escapism in the underlying swing, moodiness that pinnacles at the in-air stop-time moment after the crossover drum fill. You fall through time there. More on that later.

The bassline establishes a path to the bottom. We are going there, to the shadow. Trudging, falling, the drums heavy on the cavern floor, coming upon that which we come upon when exploring darkness. We tumble through the resistances by means of drum fills.

This is dark investigation of those specters which rise from the shadows and which we battle, which we are put here to battle, apparently. Don't get detained by the lyrics. The whole song is speaking to this alter-journey to the psyche. Because if we don't go there, we will start to lose faith, the unexplored shadow shielding us from light. We will forever believe ourselves outside of divine regard.

The solo section is the battle, of push and pull, the crashing of irregular voices that rise and fall in a perfection of antagonism.

Then, oh, the arrival to victory! The four-measure march down the streets that squares the beat and accentuates the swagger, culminating in the frolic-among-the-garlands drum fill.

We arrive back to the verse and are now emboldened for the journey, holding the torch, and, ready for the next campaign, we are now armed.

I went on my first Shamanic journey as a kind of intellectual endeavor and fell thousands of miles into the language of metaphor.

I understand metaphor. I have been blissfully falling into the written word since *See Spot Run* or something similar. When I learned to read, the images rose from the page, pictures becoming alive because of what the words were saying. When I learned to journey, I discovered the symbols of my inner world.

When we recognize that our own stories are not our full identity, we can release them from ruling us, as well as the patterns and behaviors that weight them. I found Eastern meditation practices and discovered my identity beneath stories. I found Shamanism and learned to sneak up behind the stories, unravel them in a way that allows me to clear my perception and experience life more fully.

Shamanism as I learned it is about the integrity of power. The teacher must be fully in integrity to teach integrity. I have a nose for integrity. I was yet again gifted with a great teacher in Isa Gucciardi.

Energetic integrity is even more tricky than just ethics. There are esoteric aspects to this practice, and when I began studying, I could feel the container created for the classes held strongly. This allowed me to be carried into a river of information that I had been avoiding seeing for a great deal of my life, but which felt so familiar I had to laugh. Here is where all my aspects met, where my pieces came together.

To come into integrity with one's power is to be a full container, complete, holding nothing that does not belong to you and having retrieved what you have lost. I find doing this work captivating, challenging, freeing. When working with others, I bring myself to full attention and allow the work to lead. There is a balance between holding yourself as a rigid container and allowing complete presence in awareness. I aspire to do that while drumming as well.

A shaman is someone who translates messages from the natural world to the community. The Buddha did the same, and his study of the natural world meant sensation, experience, witness. The natural world is outside us and within us. The study of one is to study the other.

Drums transmit messages as well. After the drum fill of the century at the end of the guitar solo, we hang in time. What I mean is that time elongates here, and your body, all the little muscles that hold up the bigger ones, calibrate from forward movement which pushes forward to a forward movement dropping back. It is my very favorite place in any Zeppelin song I play. So subtle, yet everything. It is like that space within the outbreath, that space before the inbreath, that stillness in the center of everything that spirals infinity in and out.

When we use the Shamanic journey as a tool for self-knowledge, there is nothing we are shown we cannot handle. The whole society at large offers a million stunning ways to avoid doing this kind of work, but once I began these internal explorations, I came upon so much freedom and light I couldn't stop. To approach healing by accessing our own knowing, recognizing there is nothing outside ourselves necessary to find wholeness, is like finding a flower endlessly blooming within us.

All great music halls in San Francisco have ghosts, as anyone who works there will tell you. It makes sense, seeing as they have been theaters for close to a hundred years, in a city rife with spookiness. All the bodies who have worked there, onstage and off, all the audiences packed in over the years, it adds up to quite a bit of plasma and energy you can feel when you walk in.

I like to think of music as a conduit connecting worlds, melodies conjuring spirits from other decades and sound-waves offering them a pathway to ride in on.

I have been inviting spirits into my body to play with me for years.

It must have started when my father died. I could feel the longing for him so often that I may have extended an invitation, inviting his energy into the physicality of the playing. This was not a conscious decision. I must have been doing this for years before I recognized it. When I play a show and fall into that center beyond time and space, there seems to be a natural opening to invitation.

Then, of course, I am playing someone else's parts onstage, getting inside of someone else's movements and body. Drumming is so much about the physical form, and in that space of no-thought, the body is a tool used by song. Time moves in a circle, opening portals. As I play, an invitation broadcasts, that others may have some use of this tool in the glory of movement that is drumming.

When I began to study Shamanic techniques later in my life, I realized that this opening is probably not the wisest thing. Probably not wise to open my energy system to invitation in a theater of drunken souls. With help, I have spent some time finding and releasing energies that are not mine to hold any longer. I get lighter and lighter over time.

This is all very esoteric and I hesitate to mention it, but no matter our own mythical cosmology, it can be of use to consider letting go of energies we have opted to carry throughout our life which no longer serve us.

They don't have to be "spirits." The benefit of finding our own internal symbolism to understand ourselves is transformative. I say I am carrying energy. Someone else may say they have a persistent memory or dream that they cannot relieve or understand. Maybe there is a feeling of something missing or something blocked. Metaphor guides us through the work of discovering our individual internal language and knowing.

I will not stop the invitation as I play. I am comfortable being a conduit now. However, I will continue to work to make sure that when the show is over, everything is in its proper place, and I walk in energetic integrity as I make my way home, ears vibrating, heart lifted in song.

54 I attended a workshop learning to assist folks in finding inner guidance. I sat next to a couple from Portland, about my age. The first day, we had superficial conversations about particulars: their trip to Berkeley, how they came to do this work.

On the second day, the man asked about my music career and said he loved music. His youngest played. He said she was fifteen years old and played the drums. "Permanently fifteen" was the way he described her, and I laughed, thinking this a description of her personality. He clarified. She had died suddenly, eight months prior.

This must be the most difficult thing a person can go through, to lose a child. I was instantly heartbroken for them. He told me the week before she passed away, she performed at a school concert in which she played "Tom Sawyer," by Rush.

It was not lost on me that a few months before this at a time of stress in my life, I too had sat down to learn "Tom Sawyer." The probability of a rock drummer attending a workshop like this, then sitting next to these kind people who had lost their rock-drummer daughter just months before—this all seemed meaningful. I had found the right place to study.

Our conversation was interrupted by an instruction to begin a Shamanic journey. I was visiting my most trusted guide, a Native American chief. The journey was led by a drum being played in the room. In the meditation, I followed the trail and sat before the guide. I was at his feet and could smell the leather on his clothing. I was amazed as always at his beauty and the feeling of guidance and protection bestowed upon me.

I noticed he was holding a beautiful white bird in his hands. It was dead, and he held it by the neck. I put my hands on it and felt its soft and gorgeous down. After a while, the chief lifted the bird and took its heart out and pushed it into my own. When he did this, I was overwhelmed by a feeling of expansion, of light, of open love, of beauty.

I see how music has informed my path to connect to a bigger truth, and I am continually overwhelmed. How is it that thirty years ago, as I picked up my first drumsticks, they would carry me here, to this unfolding of truth, connection with humanity, and to my own open heart?

55

As soon as the show started, the memory of a dream came back to me in which I was playing drums in slow motion.

In the dream, I was onstage, playing my drums, and suddenly I realized that I had the ability to set my awareness into slow motion. Everything stilled, and the feeling was exquisite. I could hit each drum so precisely in timing beyond perfection. I could see Gretchen turning slowly, and I looked directly into her eyes. I had all the time in the world to gaze into her face, to know we were in sync. Each moment, each beat, each note was ringing out exquisitely and savored. I was amazed by my new ability. I felt this was something I could always do but had just remembered.

Onstage, time spread out a little bit as it had in the dream. My playing was strong and settled in a new way. I could smell incense as my hair fell in front of my face, and I was transported to a peacefulness that had been my experience earlier in the day in meditation. I accessed joy and felt a tangible connection to my band, to the music, to the audience. It really did feel as if somehow I was playing in half time.

When we got offstage, I told the band my experience. Gretchen smiled. While she was playing, she had a thought: *How about if I try to play in half time?* We got spooked for a moment over a toast of whiskey. It makes sense we do a little mind reading onstage after so many years of playing together.

56 Behind the drums, behind my eyes, I have a sense of an area off to the left of my vision, a place wide open in stillness, clear light, a center of pure resonance. It is like a doorway. As I play, I hear a kind of invitation, like someone whispering, *Come over here.* When I approach this place, I enter light, and there is no Clem there, just awareness.

It occurred to me I could go into this light permanently. When I had this realization, I saw fear rise. My first thought was that I would go insane if I did that, or that I would tumble off the drum stool, or forget how to play. The idea of giving over completely to this energy was frightening. I seemed to be okay putting a foot in the door here and there, but I was afraid to cross the threshold. The fear became a new focus of my practice.

My whole life is practice. From unpacking the drums, to filling up the gas tank, to laughing with the band, to playing with abandon, to passing out at the end of the night, to listening to the Dalai Lama's book, to sitting and meditating and chanting *Om* in the morning . . . it is all practice. Each moment of existence, whether I am in a trance of half time or doing a shot with the bar staff, it is all part of this divine manifestation, moving ever forward.

Maybe being a rock drummer is the Clementine version of monastic life. I certainly seem to be built for movement and exertion, with a gift of stamina that may be lost in a monastery.

With challenge, we transform. My music career *is* my practice, as much as counseling and meditation and writing and driving and all the other ways I spend the moments of this life. My practice is to let go of attachment to identity, attachment to concepts, and to access the heart, to live from the heart, to live in the heart. Moment to moment, present and in truth.

Along the way, equanimity, loving-kindness, compassion, joy develop. The Four Immeasurables[11] flower and root deeper inside me. I develop ease, friendship, and gratitude as I move through music venues and put on rock shows. Music connects my heart with the hearts of others, those I know and those I know only because we are made of the same stuff, moved by the same frequencies, sharing the same space and air and molecules as we each make our way to that fearless moment when we step across that threshold, into light.

57

We were at nine thousand seven hundred feet. People were setting up an oxygen tank behind the guitar cabinet, so it was near the drums. That didn't feel right. I asked for the tank to be put inside the sound tent, out of sight of the audience. I couldn't imagine wanting to stick that mask on my face during a show and have the audience see me do it. I couldn't imagine letting go of Clementine, powerful and huge behind the drums, to become Clementine, the weakling having a hard time breathing.

"Drummers have passed out, and we've had to carry them out of here," I was told. "You're going to want the tank next to you."

From out of the dizziness, the worry, the stressing out I had been doing all day about the altitude, a strong *No* rose. *I'll* decide if I'm going to pass out during the show. *I'll* decide if I can't take it. *I'll* decide that I can be fine.

I could feel the heaviness of the big idea hanging in the air, that drumming may be too exertive for the mountain.

I don't accept your concept. If I'm going to pass out, I'm going to pass out. I'm not going to get up from the drum kit and strap that oxygen mask on me mid-set. I'm not going to let that idea of limitation win. Just, no.

Rupert Sheldrake is a scientist who writes about what he calls morphic resonance fields, fields of thought humanity creates which mold our reality. Thoughts are waves of energy, and these waves connect us.

There are all kinds of big meta concepts we buy into because we attach ourselves to these resonant thought fields. It happens on a grand scale. For instance, there are thought fields that keep us believing life is misery, or humanity must create war, or humans need competition to survive, or people are basically bad or good.

It also happens on a small scale, when someone puts the weight of their belief of what you can accomplish on you, and you not only have to fight your own battle but also the morphic resonance they are trying to pin you to.

You can tell me it isn't just a concept that I may have trouble playing drums at altitude, that it is a fact: people have been carried out on stretchers doing so. However, there are many who live at twelve thousand feet who do fine. There are folks I can see, just past the stage, hurtling down man-made snow and throwing themselves off ramps. Maybe they have been here long enough to adapt to the thin air, or maybe they are just kids, so excited and on vacation and overcome with the joy of the sport it doesn't even occur to them to feel taxed. They haven't attached themselves to the field of being compromised. So then, what are the facts? Isn't it all subject to our perception?

I treated myself all morning as if I were fragile, then decided to kindly let go of that mindset and started to see myself as perfectly capable of drumming a rock show.

I committed to playing drums with as little physical compromise as possible but then between each song I took a big gulp of water and a hopefully unnoticed drag on the small canister of oxygen I bought at the market. I breathed deeply, found the places to push and the places to catch up, and played.

If we are more empty space than matter, and our reality is created by the resistance to the energy all around us, then it really is about mind over matter. It really is about connecting to the morphic information fields giving us strength to let go of fear and to make manifest our internal power.

I accomplished the show. It wasn't the best, but by far, not the worst.

As a reward, I went up the ski lift gondola. I am laughably terrified of any conveyance involving a worn leather seat and my feet hanging over a treacherous height. I held on to the back of the seat and under the seat, and I darted my eyes side to side because I couldn't move my head. No motion at all was the only way I could handle the fear.

It was gorgeous though, and the view was the reward. I saw people going up on other gondolas, and they didn't even put down the safety bar. They sat nonchalantly, taking pictures, laughing with their friends. I couldn't connect with their freedom, but I rode the damn thing to twelve thousand feet.

I am going to choose to believe life is magnificent. It is this information field to which I am going to attach. Whenever I catch a glimpse of the outside world, the news is dire and disturbing, irritating and terrifying, and yet, I keep thinking of those big fields of information that our thoughts create, how we are together creating this reality. I keep thinking: I am going believe in the power of love. I am going to believe that along with the information fields of hate and fear, there are other, ever-widening oceans of thought connecting us to the true divinity of life.

With all the small, vocal fields of rage and unrest, a bigger field, a deeper knowing is being created at every moment. It is connecting us to a life lived in strength, without fear, discarding old concepts of separateness and scarcity that humanity has no use for. Each time a person stands up to injustice, speaks out, sacrifices safety in the name of peace, this field gets bigger. Each small act of triumph over fear builds up this field of strength. Every time we refuse to let another attach us to concepts of limitation, everybody wins.

When I was on the ski lift, my body stiff and my blood running cold each time the gondola bumped over a cable tower, I looked straight ahead, through the fear and past the terror. Reality was beauty—wide, green, sparkling, spectacular beauty. I took a deep breath of oxygen and connected right to it.

58 On a night in Arcata, we play with every intention of putting on the best show possible and then rolling out as quickly as we can.

It isn't as easy as that.

The venue is a late-night place, and even with a quick forty-minute pack of the equipment after the show, we don't get to the hotel until 2:00 a.m.

We have a 6:00 a.m. lobby call. That, combined with the adrenaline from the five-hour drive and the two-hour show, makes the night a near-sleepless one. I shower and wash the show out of my hair, a process with my tangled locks that always takes about an hour.

I lie and do the sleep meditation I have been doing all my life. I put my awareness at the top of my head, circle that awareness around the head, then down the body. I try to feel each part as my awareness circles by, and sometimes everything begins to sway, to relax, to open as awareness flows. I think I get nearly three hours of sleep, enervated but dreaming.

Six in the morning comes and the band nestles in the back of the van and goes back to sleep. I drive through the dark. The highway from the 101 to Interstate 5 is through some of the most beautiful landscape in the world, along the coast and then through the redwoods. It is a winding road, and for three hours I try my hardest to both hurry and to drive smoothly as I take the fifteen-mile-per-hour curves.

The person on the back bench has it rough. Any sudden brake will wake her. The van is a cradle I am trying not to rock. As I drive, I keep noticing when I get overly tense, and I feel my arms and hands clenched and heavy. When this happens, I breathe into my belly, holding for a moment, then breathing up and out the center channel of my body, up and out the top of my head. I rest in heart energy when I feel agitated, observe worry and tension as they rise and fall.

Meanwhile, the trees are silent and watching. I love how the redwoods hug the road. I feel a wave of sadness when I see one damaged from an accident. The mist lies heavy in the forest, and the van moans and whines as we make our way. I take my stillness from the example of the big trees. I observe a floating peace as I drive.

I turn on an audiobook chosen especially for this trip, my version of vacation lit. It is a book written by a medium, and she is speaking of how to ask loved ones to communicate with you after they die, how to ask to see a particular image to know they are close.

I don't put too much truck in all this, but I drift into a reverie of my father. What kind of symbol would I choose to ask to see, to know he was close by? Seems rather silly, and I go through the images the author suggests: rabbits, birds, deer. None of these seem particularly resonant to me and my dad. I can't imagine my father would want to take time out of wherever he is to play this game with me.

I turn a corner and brake quickly without waking anyone up. There are about twenty elk in the road, blocking my way. They are lingering there, gorgeous velvet beasts lazily moving through the fog in front of me. I wait, and a few pass the driver's window. One makes eye contact with me as he passes, a young guy with budding horns. *Hi, Dad.*

The sun finally rises when I stop for coffee and gas, and when I return to the car the sky is orange. When I reach Interstate 5, the road goes through the mountains, not nearly as winding. I set cruise control and marvel at the mist lying low in the trees. Patches of landscape look strangely white, and I realize it is ash from the summer's terrible fires, crinkling up tree branches and lying on the grass like frost. How the trees must love the mist.

59

For the first few songs of the show, I feel the long drive in my body, stiff and heavy. I tune in to my inner dialogue, and it is voicing worry. I am too tired. I drove too long. I can't play two shows. There's no way.

When I hear these thoughts, I realize my body feels fine, but my thoughts are impeding the playing. When I run my awareness from head to toe, I feel perfectly strong and able. The thoughts are causing me stress, summoning that heavy feeling as I play.

I sink in, follow my breath to the bottom of the self and start listening to the music, getting inside the songs and letting go of thought. Where there is tension, I send breath, which opens and lubricates. Where there is dread, underneath is joy. I play well. It occurs to me that I used to use so much force to make these shows happen. Now it is absence of force that sustains my power.

The last two songs of the second set, I acknowledge that my body is tired. I hold the sticks more like a caveman than a drummer, and I am all hunched over the snare drum. It feels good like that. I keep trying to sit up straight, but my body is tired of supporting my big head. We end and I am happy, a feeling of accomplishment.

I have very little ability for conversation, but I get to say hello to several happy rockers and relax into the long end-of-the-night process: breaking down the drums, packing the equipment into the van, getting paid, rounding everyone up, driving to the hotel.

The gentleman behind the hotel desk is delightfully cheery and tells me there are eagles and other wildlife who show up in the morning. It smells so good, dripping trees and a small lake. The band has a congratulatory drink, and I know I can sleep until 11:00 a.m.

In the morning, I rise and check in with that part of me that watches. It is always there, infinite, open, receiving what is. I go drink coffee and summon eagles.

KASHMIR

In "Kashmir," Led Zeppelin offers hypnosis as mood. The drums are a trance, with that magical hidden syncopation implied under the drum pattern. I play it live a little differently than Bonham played it on the record. His version is a study in restraint all the way through. I like to play it big in the choruses, splashing back and forth between cymbals and rolling around the toms in a way he did not do.

Most of all, I think of the movement of camels and the swish of desert, even though after a few years of playing this song I ended up finding out that Kashmir is not in the desert at all but a gorgeous mountain range. Typical American.

I still feel a Bedouin in my conjuring for this song, the slow unveiling that comes over ceaseless days of travel.

Travel was so important for me, and still is, but not to the same degree it was when I set off for Portugal at twenty-two years old with eight hundred dollars and a one-way ticket, or through my years of exploration of the great American landscapes.

For the time being, it is the stationary travel that most holds its charm.

My window seat lives in a little porch room off the kitchen. I imagine that one day the whole room will topple over in an earthquake, set on stilts as it is. We've got bedrock beneath us, and the house has weathered such rattling since the early 1900s, but I still have a plan to leap into the kitchen and roll beneath the table should the shaking begin.

You are supposed to practice disaster routes so the shock of crisis doesn't leave you paralyzed. I don't go as far as leaping around and spoiling my comfortable perch, but I spend a little time imagining the tuck and roll before I forget all that and fall in love all over again with the breeze.

The problem with practicing for disaster is that there are so many disasters you just don't see coming. When I was a child, my mother was in a car accident. Someone hit the station wagon in the middle of an intersection. I don't remember much except my sister and her friends flying around in the back seat, the car off-kilter in the middle of the road. My mother told me to run to a store to call my father, and there is a vague memory of my surprise that I could not remember my father's number once I got there. I see myself running back and forth a couple of times, forgetting the number each trip.

Maybe it was the first time I could not rely on my brain. It was impossible to remember the number and impossible to properly communicate other than to say there had been a car accident. As I flailed, I was also amazed at the detachment of those in the store, who seemed annoyed and were decidedly unhelpful as, standing confusedly, I tried to remember and then returned to the car.

In Shamanic practice, there is a belief that when there is a shock or trauma a piece of us detaches and stays in the trauma. This part of ourselves, which is called a soul part, remains behind in order to allow us to move forward. The result is the dazed detachment of shock, as if you had just shaken loose a piece of yourself and now are empty of tools on which you usually rely.

Somewhere, then, a part of me has been running back and forth in that intersection for all these years, confused and amazed that what I always depended on, my mind and my ability to remember and think, had gone.

As we move through our lives, we leave these parts of ourselves behind in all moments of trauma, small and large. As we age, the missing parts begin to cause problems, and we become more aware of missing something important, something left behind.

Most of our misery comes from our attempts to fill this emptiness with things we think might make us whole. For me, it has been a hunger for knowledge, a hunger for movement, a hunger for accomplishment, hunger for food and indulgence and spiritual progress, and so many other things it would take me weeks to list.

Some look to ensure they will never experience that dazed feeling again, and they let fear rule. To make sure they will never find themselves in that kind of trauma again, they feed the emptiness with fear, build walls, avoid life. I have done this too.

Maybe those things we reach for become specific to what was lost: I have both sought to amplify that dazed feeling in various ways, as well as identified myself with my brain's abilities. My life has been spent feeling that it was important to be important in some way, maybe so if I had to ask for help again, people would listen.

I wonder how many other accidents happen in that intersection, with the energy of that little lost Clem running around. I better get to work to retrieve that part, just in case it is causing some bother for others, not to mention for my own healing. For we can retrieve those parts left behind, fill up those holes and bring ourselves into wholeness. That is what the shamans do and what we can do too. I think of the tradition on Bali, a part of their culture, leaving candies where people have stumbled to appease the spirits.

When I see pictures of California from the 1970s, I remember those seaside drives up the 101, the hills so empty of development. I love that feeling of openness, space, and time. A movie reel plays in my mind as the breeze picks up.

Children without seatbelts. Station wagons made of steel. Ramshackle sandwich shacks. Pay phones.

One thing I love about travel is the way you see your life from a distance as you move through landscapes, through cities and countrysides. You can't help but examine all the patterns of your life, set out before you like the rows of farm plots and the subtle order of mountain ranges. In all the movement, the mind becomes quiet and reflective, and perspective rises as if you're looking in a mirrored pool.

To find ourselves in altered-state work, it is like this. We move through landscapes of our interior. Here, we meet beings of pure love, parts of ourselves ringing truth. Everyone we meet here has our best interests at heart. No wonder I walk in gratitude through my days. Somehow, I was led to travel this world inside of me and found a field of love.

From this field, struggle feels fair and equitable. I see into that which is blocking me while trying to protect me, or that which is not mine to hold.

The drum leads the way. The drum leads us to the inside, the journey to light which frees the darkness.

I don't know one unkind thing to say about this gorgeous day. The breeze carries its own hypnosis. A sailboat drifts in the distance, following the line of rooftops between the house and the Bay. I think of moving from this place, but I have never found any other place that plays with light and shade like San Francisco.

How soft the air, how green the trees and flower bushes. The mockingbird has been going crazy all day, so insistent. He sits in the fig tree below and I see that the loquats have fruited. This makes me happy, since it means the parrots will be along in the next month, and that is always a raucous event. Their little green bodies and red faces drive me crazy with delight.

When the traveling stills, we come home.

6 1 A robin on a wire surveys the little park. The robin's song is so pretty and lilting, but at the end a little rasp scrapes out. I never knew the robin's song could be so pretty. Maybe the harsh ending clouded my whole perspective of it. The push at the end adds a kind of desperation that solidifies poignancy. I feel it directed at me. He is a fat robin. I am enchanted with his orange breast against the clear blue of the sky.

I see one of my blue jays. It is one of the pair who cavort in the garden outside my window seat glass, I just know. I see him dancing in the crimson bougainvillea, hopping on the bulging wall of red and green. He is playing a game, happy. He looks back at me, finds an exit, disappears through it.

There are crows all day. One swoops low through the park, braying as it flies and then lifting high over the gate and beyond. *As the crow flies.* That phrase comes into my head, and I feel a sense of envy for traveling so. His bombast agitates two doves. I feel the air pulse with their fluttering.

I gaze at the water in San Francisco Bay and ponder its relation to the color wheel of sky. I turn a corner, and the sun is the largest thing in view, hanging heavy over the bell curve of Chestnut Street, burning behind the marine layer and spreading a coral light across the screen door of sky.

I come back from whatever thought has pulled me away, to sound. Again, there are crows. They fly overhead, their calls a fading alarm. I switch up my attention and start to play with listening. My eyes follow the sidewalk so I may listen intently to every layer of sound: the heavy whoosh of a tour bus, the whining of the engine and the sharp cry of brakes, the conversation of teenagers. Tires sigh on the street beyond, and my clothing rustles against my limbs in motion. The sound of the breeze is in my hair, a small white-noise buzz in my ears, and still, on a level all to themselves, the crows.

I return to the house and sit in meditation. One crow interrupts with a persistent squawk. What is he doing out there, in the courtyard where there are never crows, outside the window of my little room? It stops me for a while, unsettles me. I think they are the messenger birds. Is there something I am to know?

In meditation, I sink deeply and watch thoughts try to steal me away. I find it easy to let them pass unnoticed, but there is something out of reach, something I can tell I am trying to find, a way of *not* trying I cannot reach. I sit for an hour or so, and at the end I am restless and give up. When I first sit, I am overwhelmed by a rising, a silver bubble of emptiness growing and evaporating my physical body. I focus on the feeling, and it goes away. I am left in a still space where battle enters and releases, enters and releases.

One thing I have learned is what I don't understand now often makes some sense later, so I just let it go. Maybe later, a conversation will spread some light on the struggle of that hour of meditation. This is the message, to accept what is. More information will unfold or withhold, this too a message.

As I rest here, it occurs to me to look, really look. I see the red carpet, the diffused afternoon light, the movement of the candle flames and the waving loquat leaves in the periphery of vision. The wooden chimes clatter and the pug snores, and what will stay in my memory is most likely the smell of fresh Bay air, a light of perfect happiness that will sustain me through less happy times no doubt to come. As the 3:00 p.m. church chimes move through me, I breathe.

62 I put my attention at the top of my head, and as my mind travels slowly down, my skin dissolves until I am a mass of small, vibrating balls. When awareness reaches my toes, I sit in the delight of vibration. The me who is the observer flies around, observing this mass of molecules, and as a rain shower hits the roof of the meditation hall, I see sound waves ripple through with a sweet shudder.

There is a small cluster of molecules where I know my hip to live, and I recognize it as pain without any sensation of such. I fly around the cluster, and as I observe, the balls loosen and separate and let go of each other. I am completely neutral as I watch.

I am observing pain without the physical sensation of it.

I have read about the great awakening moments of people, of the ego cracking in two as awareness falls thousands of miles into the true self, or of the flash of light in which the unity of all being changes reality forever. My insight a few weeks ago was that maybe that's not how it will be for me. Maybe mine will be an endless unfolding, a slow peeling back of each flower petal of realization. Maybe for me it will take lifetimes before I experience awakening. Maybe each time I allow myself to get caught up in this life the flower grows more petals.

Let what comes come.
Let what goes go.
Find out what remains.[12]

The Clementine ego who talks too much and who has that whiskey shot and who gets annoyed and who says the wrong thing and who gets snarky and who forgets the phone charger and who screws up "Babe I'm Gonna Leave You" because she's thinking about her kick drum pedal and forgets to count, here, in this still morning, gets swallowed up in the sea at the base of the true self. Here, the stillness. Here, the infinite. Nothing lost. Nothing changing. The idea of having to start over on the path seems like a funny concept of a hollow reality.

Starting, stopping, even these concepts blow away in the light of the eternal. When I find this expansive and expanding energy, I see how Clementine keeps inserting herself: fears, attachments, concepts. I witness those intrusions, little clouds that blow through. I watch them evaporate as I open to this spacious awareness.

How hard she always is on herself. She thinks that a week of socializing can reduce the power of what she already knows. She thinks she can possibly damage any progress made on her path. She thinks and judges and worries and regrets and feels defeated. Linearity is persistent and stubborn.

Meanwhile, the still consciousness of all awakened beings past, present, and future animates this turbulent reality she rockets through.

63

In the big park. We lie for a while in a respectable manner. Then, the pug becomes obsessed with other picnics. I get tired of his wanderings and begging for more treats, so we get up and ramble around.

The death-wish pug snaps at a Husky in the dog run area, so we take our business to the top of the park, where the big trees moan and squeak. There is a configuration of several branches the wind sets to crying every time I am at the top of this hill. The white eucalyptus branches must be rubbed raw by now in this frictional embrace. Still, they seem to shriek with joy.

The sun is warm and we have no place to go, so when we get to the other side of the hill, rather than leave, I throw the blanket down among the buttercups and fling myself there on my stomach, back to the heat of the sun. Big trees sing. I give the pug one last salmon treat and he gobbles it down and then lolls in the grass. I can tell he's surprised at his fortune to get to stay a while longer in the park, the place he loves so dearly.

I don't take my shoes off. I lie there, the leash around my wrist as the dog traipses back and forth over me to find his position. He rests next to my leg, needing contact. I listen to the leaves: frantic cheering, then soft.

In the background I hear the wide drone of city, and I imagine the weight of ocean hitting sand, miles away. Just how far can I hear, really? I investigate the auditory levels, separating the sounds into tiers: the voice of a woman speaking to her child, a siren very far away, airplanes, jet and propeller. Car tires, a dog barking, some manner of machinery, digging or drilling.

I see waveforms of sound as if I am looking into my music editing program, and I place the different frequencies in my mind's eye so they shimmer or undulate like wind currents higher or nearer above. There is the very high whistle of tinnitus up with the feather-white clouds. Here beneath me, the low moan of the earth, heavy with the weight of population. Which sound travels farthest to reach my hearing?

I think of the earthquake waves that move quickly side to side and scatter out with first shot, then the long, land-shifting vertical waves that upend earth. In the magic light of San Francisco, the promise of catastrophe deepens all color.

It has been slow going for me, recognizing birdsong in this city. I know the crows of course, and the jays, the twit of the hummingbird, the robins, the parrots. The sharp yelp I hear might be finch cry. I don't know what those mottled black birds prancing near us in the grass sing.

Parrots fly overhead in a pandemonium, and they stagger en masse noisily across the sky of the park. They always seem as though they're arguing as they go. They blink in and out of the air, still-frame animation flipping pages across the sky.

I lose all sound in tree song again, then silence, then birdsong. Circular, rhythmic breath of the day, flowing across me as the sun gets too hot. Then, dissolution of thought and of naming. Can I listen and not name?

There is a current of water that sits at the perfect depth for the pressure of sea above and below to form a transmitting wave. Like a radio signal, it can send whale song far distances. When scientists traveled to some of the lowest depths of the ocean, they thought to put a microphone on top of the craft. They were shocked to hear a loud and cacophonous din, with little idea of the source of any of the sounds.

My meditation practice often starts with sound. First, the sound of a chime or a bell instantly stills and opens my mind. I follow the ring down the well of silence, the absence of the gone bell. I look for places of no sound. Stillness. The most difficult place to find is the space without language. Sometimes, I hear the word *Awareness!* as I search, and laugh with frustration. My head spins. My body tenses. What am I trying to do, anyway? Why am I trying at all?

I let go. I let go of this internal brain conversation and exist beneath language, beneath sound, beneath sense and body. Awareness of awareness.

64

When I get close to the edge of the Presidio, the scent of eucalyptus overwhelms me, and I am filled with an old feeling of home. In one of the backyards of my childhood, big silver-dollar trees littered the patio with their dusty disks, and the smell was like this menthol. It is a primary California scent for me. Here at the end of the street, a whole forest waves the fragrance past the buttercream mansions and the immaculate vista. My past and my present merge in the smell of the trees.

It is a warm, cloudless day, and the water of the Bay is a blue sky on which islands float. I come upon a hummingbird, sipping from the pink and white salvia. An arm's length away, he is lost in a dream of nectar, so I get close to his chubby body, his glittering copper head, his impossibly iridescent green belly.

I hear a high twit from a branch and see a sparrow needling for attention. In fact, as I stand on the landing between the steps up and down, bird sound is cacophonous. I hear a jay far above, and there are so many dragonflies. Their greeting hums close to my ears. A yellow warbler rises from brush trees like a caped crusader and lifts to a tall branch for a moment, perched and buzzing his funny call, then he dances away with a compadre. They're off to fight crimes together, or to commit them, through the high castles of the neighborhood.

There are a few folks running up the steps, headphones on, and I marvel at their dedication to such physical exertion. Their hearts must be strong and noble, a revelation of function and purpose, efficient machines moving this other machine to the top. Next time I play drums, I will remember to adore my heart for a while.

I walk down the steps and am lost looking in windows, up driveways, into door glass, across landings, where I see rooms bathed in view. I will always believe that to live in such a masterpiece of architecture, life must spill out from moment to moment in a fresh and melon-y way, crisp as white wine.

The breeze blesses me as I walk to the bottom of the hill. There is such a narrow window of temperature in San Francisco, a sliver of options enabling homeowners to paint a house pink with bright creamed cornices with no danger of deterioration of luster. The sky spends its time playing with contrast.

65

When the Dalai Lama said goodbye to John Oliver at the end of an interview, His Holiness took John Oliver's hand and pressed it to his cheek in the most tender, loving, and sweet way. In that action, the delicate expression of love for the other. John Oliver startled and collapsed in delight.

How wonderful to startle those you encounter with a simple motion conveying unconditional connection. Can I find my own ways to startle the world with my love? Can I lose myself in love for the other, in that clear light, resting in the center of us all?

I was holed up during a period when the Old Man and the pug were out of town, and I had a couple of weeks between shows. I was sequestered by my own choosing. After a couple of days, I ventured out of the house to get supplies.

Walking home after my interaction at the corner store, it became apparent how much my mood had lifted with the contact of other humans. Maybe it was the meditation I had been engaged in that allowed me to notice this, but it was abundantly clear how much lighter my mood, how tingly my whole physical being, after short conversations with strangers.

I had been happy during my time at home, not missing anything, but with this remarkable boost in an already good mood, I saw how important it is that I be with my kind. It was like the revelation offered by the pug's trainer that made me rue the ways we had treated our dogs when I was growing up. Dogs need to see their own kind once a day to feel healthy and happy.

I am a pack animal too, I guess. For all my love of being interior, it is the external world that enlivens me.

A musician is a funny kind of career for someone so happy living a contemplative life. I have often wondered if the reason I started playing music was so I could be in social situations and still have a job to do. Having a purpose makes it easier to be in the world. Maybe that's why I became a bartender long ago and why being onstage is more comfortable than being in the audience. Maybe to spend my time qualifying purpose would be worth my while.

66 We think meditation must be so formal. There is something important about sitting with intention, but we are never separate from the marvelous tool of our breath that brings us right here. We can do this all day long, this awareness of breath.

When we focus this way, we discover that somehow, in most of our moments, all is well. Another of my great teachers, Joe Loizzo, offered a metaphor of finding a town crier walking the streets of our interior, calling out, *All is Well, All is Well.* When we arrive in our moments, we realize there is a part that is well, no matter what else is going on.

Even through trauma and sorrow, even through pain and worry, this part of us calls out. We can listen deeply by following our breath to this place. Just the fact that our breath is working signals that all is indeed well. Our blood is flowing. Our heart is beating. Molecules rearranging. Our mind is allowing thoughts to rise and beneath this conception of bad and good is that hum of knowing. All is well.

How would it be to expand this out, to the world? It has become so normal to say, *Everything is crap.* Inequity, misery, illness and war and death and countless problems that seem to signal the end of something. It doesn't feel right to even consider there could be another way of viewing things. To see things as "okay" makes us feel as if we are ignoring problems, glossing over suffering, putting our heads in the sand.

Our society has become a place in which to say that all is well makes us feel naive or guilty. It is important for us to recognize what is working and peaceful. There must be an energy in the center, a moderating well-being here between poles of terrible and ignorant. By cultivating this feeling of okay-ness, it expands. Feeling good is a generative energy. Our perception can change our experience and our actions.

We might realize this same field of the night watchman existing in our greater reality. Is there hum beneath the surface, a steady rhythm of breath in, breath out, that the whole of the planet experiences at all times, no matter the dire situation being experienced? Beneath all the chaos, is all well?

We can most clearly find peace in nature. The plants and trees and flowers are a reminder of this still and peaceful thriving, this neutrality. The sky is movement of wind and water, and the ground, cradle and vitality. When we merge our awareness with sky and earth we find stillness, hear the soft peal of the lamplighter's bell. In the city, the weed grows between the cracks of our awareness, and we zoom in through chaos and see the flower. In the earth of the battlefield, teeming growth thrives in the soil below.

We can let go of believing we are separate from the underlying grace at the top and bottom of each breath. Then, we are strong enough to meet what lies between.

67 There is a kind of pain in opening your heart to beauty. Maybe the pain comes in imagining the loss of the thing you are loving. The precariousness of earth and sky, the tenuous relation of humanity with nature. The constantly changing landscapes we love, moment to moment and year to year. The dance will dance the final step, and the stage will go dark.

Or maybe, the poignancy is of the inability to truly possess, the ache of our own longings. The song spins out in the darkened room, and we will never write something as moving or perfect. The poem is perfect. I will never write something as beautiful as those three lines.

We drop ourselves into beauty, and our own mortality gets spotlit. How will I live up to this perfection? Maybe this beauty only shines a light on my failings and inabilities, and in that sense, it is too painful to look at. Should I avoid looking directly at the sunset so as not to see my own inadequacies illuminated?

Is the prosaic life less painful? Is a life lived never moved by beauty less painful than caring that I may never achieve a single moment of such perfection?

Or will I volunteer to be hurt over and over and over? Here I see myself reflected, my heart opening wider and wider, hurt deeper and deeper by my own inabilities, but in the opening, I see this too is beautiful.

I long for the ribbons of light to bare my heart to the sky, all of beauty, all of nature. I long for the song spilling into the room to lay bare my romantic heart and love completely the depth of which humanity is capable. I long to forever be that strange lady in the audience, freely weeping. Beauty, lay heavy on my heart and tear the self to shreds. I will be wide open until I die.

SINCE I'VE BEEN LOVING YOU

68

"Since I've Been Loving You," a perfect expression of the same sentiment by four individual voices. John Paul Jones dropping into the deep, carrying us with him. Jimmy Page bereft and trying to buck up. Robert Plant at full sadness rainbow.

And Bonham. There is a forlornness in the album take I will never get over. I have a sense that the nakedness here is not what he wants to show us but impossible to contain. God, what a song. No one since has done it like this. That is a band, right there. Same emotion, four ways of expressing it.

I really love Bonham's working-man approach underneath the guitar solo. It is a squared-off *fuck it I'm going to just get it done* attitude that I feel in every part of me. He makes a valiant effort to transform the emotion he's shown us and tries to prove his strength to overcome.

There is such beauty there, an artist allowing us to watch as he comes to terms with emotion and the route he takes through it. He moves into flamboyant desperation, the acting out. In the end, the joy of drumming meets him. The drums call attention to themselves, transport us.

There is one image I remember every year at the holidays, that of my father untangling Christmas lights. I was about eighteen years old, and I happened to be in the back yard when, through the window, I saw him sitting in the living room, my little sister sitting next to him, the big pile of colored lights reflecting on his face.

I don't know why I stopped and imprinted this moment on my consciousness. I stood there for a while and watched. His face was oddly peaceful, and the weight of his deep domestic spirit sort of fell on me. At this point in my story, we rarely got along, my teen angst frustrating to him, his authoritarian personality angering me constantly. But at this moment, I saw him clearly with a deep compassion. I felt his love for the family, for the rituals of family life that gave his life meaning. I understood him as I gazed into his face without him knowing, seeing ripples of frustration at the tangle of lights and the stern acceptance of his duty to untangle them. My little sister was sitting quietly and watching, asking him questions, pulling him gruffly out of his reverie.

I never could reach him. From the time I stopped being a small child I was closer to him through that pane of glass than I was with him. All our emotions and assumptions, his gruffness and my pride, all the frustration of what we wanted the other to be—was there ever a moment of pure communication? He loved me so much he sacrificed his dreams for mine. I loved him so much I always reached to shine some glory onto his sacrifice. All of this is story, all of this is so far from true connection that it is as if we didn't know each other at all.

No matter how close we get there is no touching anyone. We reach to the singularity of connection, knowing we find infinity there. We gaze through a fog of story and emotion. We reach and yearn for union and never seem to break through the narrative we are telling ourselves about the person for whom we reach. No wonder at the holidays, when we are supposed to feel the most love, many people feel the saddest.

This inability to connect happens when we see those around us through the lens of our own ego, our own story. This inability to connect happens when we are looking for something separate from ourselves, never seeing that we are all the same substance, with one base. We reach and yearn and strive for intimacy when we are not separate.

I regret all the ways I have not connected to my family and to those I have loved. I regret all the ways I have kept people at a distance. Even when I love them enough that I would sacrifice my life for theirs, I can never seem to get close enough. During the holidays I miss my family, yet when I am with them, I can't figure out how to get close to them, to convey the profound love I feel. There is only this poignant reaching and inability. I worry that they will never know my love for them, and this worry separates us even more. My family is so free with their love. I think, *If my heart breaks a little at the holiday, how agonizing the pain of those who feel loved less.*

Yet here, in this infinite plain, we are love. We are communion. When I let go of all the story, all the memory, all the projection of the future, all my own wants and needs and ideas, there is only this still place. I can love people as they are, not as I would have them be.

I bring humanity into my heart, and the love I feel spreads out beyond my body, beyond the room, beyond the stars and planets, beyond the universe, this place that never reaches the singularity of "I love you." This is what we are.

I am looking through the window at my father. I am my father. I am the window. I am the light, shining into his face, first red, then green, then white.

69 I dreamed I was sitting at a table of elders. I asked of my faceless company, what was the purpose of my life. A voice in my ear thundered so loudly it woke me: "To learn how to love."

This startled me as I rose. I can say with confidence I have never had that thought before. Love has never seemed like something I had to figure out. I am fortunate that love comes easily, and it has in my life, both from me and to me. What did that mean, to learn how to love?

Then, practicing a Tibetan meditation exercise guiding me to a place where I was to accept a feeling of being unconditionally loved, I was shocked to realize I couldn't.

I have had a laughably loving life, with openhearted family and friends, and still I seemed to be incapable of feeling so loved. Whenever I got close in the meditation to feeling this love emanating from another being, my mind flew away, into the past or future, into chaos. It literally ran away in terror.

This realization upset everything I knew of myself.

I thought, *But I love others unconditionally. I can easily feel this for others, so why can't I accept it for myself?*

Here I found that belief of "not enough." Not loveable, not good, not good enough.

After a while of examining this, I came to let go of what was blocking this feeling. Little by little, I allowed the incredible warmth and comfort of feeling unconditionally loved to flood my system. It was transformative.

Then came the realization that what I had been calling unconditional love for others was not this, no matter how expansive it had felt. Loving "unconditionally" was attached to a need to be someone who could love this way.

You always hear, in order to love you must first learn to love yourself. I guess this is what that's all about. All I know is once I could accept feeling loved unconditionally myself, the way I feel about others changed too.

I always thought of love as easy, but the dream is right. I am learning it. Not in a self-help sort of way, since the personality self is beyond learning love, will always have some barrier erected which it uses to shield itself. I am learning to accept that the self which is not Clementine, this other ocean of awareness below attachment, *is* pure love. I am learning to accept the love of the consciousness or vibration or energy that set me into form. Learning to love with no attachment to the loving, truly needing nothing in return, living in the light of it.

What would it be like to love unconditionally? Love the emotion is not what is required for this state. An emotion always has an opposite, and to depend on the *emotion* love is to eventually fail. Emotion wanes, changeable. We no longer find the warm feelings of the beginning of the relationship, or we become so attached to the way the emotion felt at an earlier time that how it appears later becomes unbearable.

The love required to love unconditionally is energy, not emotion. It is the open, neutral, boundless, and radiant energy at the bottom of our self. In this field, love energy expands exponentially; in fact, there seems to be no beginning or end. There is no requirement of the other and no ego to be hurt or needy. It accepts completely.

Often, we think by loving this way, we become a pushover, used by others who could take advantage of this openness.

Yet, living in this truth of self, boundaries are true as well. Energy is not spent on reacting and attacking. There is no ego to create a barrier to understanding, and relationship becomes painless.

Even when the other you are loving is closed off to this energy, even if a person feeds on conflict and problems, the energy of compassion shows the right path of action. Maybe it is time to let this person continue on without you. Maybe you let them go. When this decision is done from a place of unconditional love, then suffering is alleviated by knowing this is the right course of action for all. Truth carries us through.

In old structures of relationship, I will always disappoint you. I will always be selfishly fighting for what my ego needs: to be respected and cherished and cared for and left alone. Yet, in the energy of love, there is no one to coddle. I am here to celebrate you as I celebrate me. What is best for you is all I am. We are one being and the delight of two solitudes, meeting, protecting, greeting each other.[13]

When you have a taste of this energy in a personal relationship, it is not so big a jump to imagine what the whole world would be like in this field. How would unconditional love in the world look, meeting enemies with compassion and a desire for understanding, letting go of the concepts of right and wrong and good and evil based on the past? Just truth.

The ego fears this. The whole world fears this but then I let this concept go with all the rest of it. All I can do is to let go of fear, dive in.

70

A favorite video of mine is of Vernon Howard, whom I laughingly see as a spiritually awakened Karl Malden:

Think of the phrase "a wave of pain." You've had them, huh? How many today? Five hundred? They're uncountable. Because you're not aware of what's going on inside of you down at the office, at the home, driving your car. One day alone, you've had hundreds . . . You're home, you're washing the dishes or cooking dinner. All of the sudden a great dreadful feeling comes over you. You remember something from the past, or you think of something that you have to face next week. While cooking that dinner, peeling those carrots, right in the middle of that, that wave of anguish comes over you, gives you a heavy spirit and a very sober, sad face, and you're all alone in the house, let's say, and no one knows that that feeling overcame you, that that wave went through you. Not even you know that it's happened. There is no way I can overestimate, overjudge, the importance of you knowing what is going on inside of you every second . . . Moment by moment awareness of a wave of pain is the first type of recognition that is essential if you're ever going to change anything. You cannot change anything before you first see it.[14]

After I watched this, I closed my eyes and observed. Sure enough, undulating waves of sensation responded to every thought rising. Once I focused in, they became so apparent and so numerous I started to feel sympathy for myself. Poor Clem, walking around with this rolling agony rippling through her body for so many years. Even after all these years of mindfulness meditation, the number of these twinges was astonishing. Even sound triggered them. My ego thinks it should not have to be subjected to construction noise.

Once I got over marveling at these waves, I sat and further observed. I realized I could use each sensation as a tool. Being led by physical sensation into neutrality seems to be easier than trying to work with thought. Thoughts grow so exponentially it can be difficult to let go of them, to let go of believing we *are* our thoughts. Recognizing a slight wave of nausea or a clutching heaviness in my chest is much easier. I don't attach to explanation. I ignore the story the ego tries to tell, and I deal with the sensation of it. I follow the wave into expansive peace.

What happens is: a thought comes. I observe the wave of uncomfortable physical sensation in the body. I allow all the thoughts and emotion to rise and release. I find the place underneath sensation, the ocean of neutrality at the base. The physical sensation pushes me into neutrality.

When I recognized that the body was a gift, an instrument through which I could find the field of the divine, everything shifted. I began to understand how it was possible to love.

Sirriya lives in upstate New York. She has been a part of my life since I was twenty-two years old, when I was living in New York City and bouncing like a ping-pong ball from identity to identity. She was my teacher from the moment we met. I wanted to know what she knew, the easy and joyful way of being in the world, the seeking mind, the deep knowing. I wanted to be on the same path. I was too naive to know what that meant, but it was instinct to follow her influence. I wanted to learn how to laugh like that.

We now joke about being from the same planet. On our planet, the view of reality is rarefied and illusory. We communicate with animals, and there is an appreciation for birds. A sort of laissez-faire attitude toward life prevails, yet at the same time we are deeply invested in the big picture. We were put here on this planet in these bodies, and we assume that whatever put us here will care for us. We are ready for whatever that means. Even death, in which neither of us believe. There is a streak of joy running through beings from our planet that makes itself known early on in childhood and which makes itself more apparent as life persists.

I welcome her teachings with a heart that opens so much I can't imagine it opening more, yet still there is so much to learn. She laughingly catches me in my traps of mind and story. We tell tales of the past only to release them forever. We both feel a sense of speaking of someone else when we revisit our lives before now, even the one we have shared.

I felt delivered to her doorstep by fate, on a Christmas Eve long ago. Now, I am again delivered to her doorstep, and with every visit I awaken more. During the days of my visits, nothing much happens. We quickly fall into sync. I drive her around in her cluttered white car, we coordinate our food and sleep patterns, and we spend a great deal of time with her family of cats. It is easy, and I wonder what it is like for people who are strongly attached to their personalities and who need things to be just so. It seems like you wouldn't ever get to relax like this. A visit with her is a feeling of floating. Meanwhile, the whole time, I am learning. Learning to let go of the contractions, learning to take power away from the things that try to steal my attention.

She asked me to bring up ideas and situations in my life that I have given power to. Body image, identity, financial situation. I played with setting each issue out in front of me and taking the power back. As I did this, I felt my center open wide and fill with a renewed strength that was also no strength. Letting go.

Two days after a visit to New York, my mother arrived in San Francisco in the middle of a raging heat wave. It had been too long since I had seen her, and I begged her to come. I won the family lottery at birth. I look forward to seeing my mother and sisters so much I become fluttery before their arrival.

My mother has come to visit me at many iterations of my life. She visited the college-student me and rode around on my boyfriend's scooter and was one of the girls. She visited the studio apartment in Seattle where she slept in the closet. Now, on a miserably hot day, she traveled in the band van to a festival south of San Francisco, watching me set up my drums with concern.

We both got heatstroke and spent Sunday on the couch, watching movies and trying to feel better. With my mom, even this was a blessing, as we got to just hang out, not run around San Francisco looking at stuff. We lay beneath the fan, side by side on the couch, together. Even feeling crummy, my mom is joyful, easy, light, funny, and noncomplaining.

When I was a teen, my mother's positive outlook drove me crazy. I was reading Rimbaud and Camus and Dostoevsky, and life seemed so much wider and darker than she knew. I thought I knew so much better with my dark vision of the world. Now, I only aspire to her way of being, this lighthearted way of meeting her moments, seeing no point in dwelling in darkness.

In times of difficulty, I see her batten down, get ferocious. When she was ill many years ago, I saw her set her jaw and meet the illness with a kind of steel will. Then, after it was over, this happy spirit bounced back and prevailed. She is happy at her center. What else could you wish in a life?

These two women, Sirriya and my mother, just a few years apart in age, are currents. I am a buoy, carried along the river, sometimes pulled under, sometimes caught in the turbulence. These influences carry me along, both joyful, both awakened in their own ways. One carries me along the path of profound knowing. One shows me that simplicity in being is the key.

I eat up stories of Ram Dass and other seekers from generations ago who traveled to far lands to find their gurus. There is the story of Robert Thurman, how when he arrived at the house of his guru his legs stopped working as he walked up the driveway, the anticipation of the meeting so profound. I love the stories of the instant knowing, the overwhelming connections, the lightning bolt when finding what you have been seeking without even knowing you were looking. Neem Karoli Baba manifesting as an old man on a train, guiding students to him. Ramana Maharshi traveling to Arunachala Mountain, knowing beyond knowing that this was the incarnation of his guru. Yogananda seeing his guru down an alleyway and recognizing him instantly.

I guess it doesn't happen so dramatically all the time. I guess what happens for many of us is that our teachers are around us already, and often we get them at birth. Sometimes teachers are found in a series of circumstances that make for a great story later on. Sometimes, you realize that the people in your life have already been teaching you the most profound truths all along: joy, faith, and above all, unconditional love.

72   I spent a week binge-watching the show *Naked and Afraid.*

The name of the series says it all, but in case you haven't tuned in, a man and a woman are set down in an intense natural environment—the swamps of Louisiana, the jungles of Peru, the plains of Namibia—without a shred of clothing and only a machete and, if they've chosen wisely, a fire starter. They meet as they pick their way through their new environment in their birthday suits. Then, they live for twenty-one days together, after which they trek to a rescue spot several miles away.

Snakes, spiders, crocodiles, hippos, soooo many bugs. Killer bees. Sand flies. Panthers. Elephants. I watch in fascination and have learned some things.

First, don't get fancy with fire making. Get a flint and do that first or you are going to get cranky. Second, do not drink water without boiling it. Ever. Raise your shelter off the ground. Store firewood somewhere dry for when the rains come. Which they always do.

Bugs want to eat you. It seems they are more of a danger than snakes, which is surprising to me. I thought if you came upon a snake, you could pretty much kiss life goodbye, but apparently, it is pretty easy to outwit a deadly snake and have him for dinner. Sand flies, on the other hand, will cause more problems for you than anything you can imagine.

Also, how on earth can these people walk around without shoes? I walk down the tiled hallway of my apartment building to get the mail and am hobbled by tiny stones. I did not know that jungles have four-inch needle spikes littering the ground. Good grief.

Anyway, the real addictive part of the show, as is the case with most reality TV, is the naked, pardon the pun, window into the human psyche.

After four days of intense heat, panic trying to find water, building a shelter, sleepless nights, and bugs, most people ditch the initial positive attitude. Then, they begin to find fault with their partners. At four days, folks get hungry, and all vision turns outward to blame. He's lazy. She's a princess. I wish I had any other partner but him.

If the couple makes it to the end of the challenge, there has come a point when they are forced to apologize for all the mean things said during the blame period: *you stink, you're stupid, I hate you!* Many a player eats crow—figuratively, thankfully—and realizes they have to suck it up and get along if they are to survive.

It is enlightening to watch this play out from a distance, because we get to see both sides of the conflict. She thinks he's lazy. He thinks she's stupid for expending so much energy. Aren't they both kind of right? The whole time you're thinking, why don't you tell him how you're feeling? Why do you have to be so closed off and stubborn? You see the damage of the past. She's never felt validated. He's always been uncomfortable with emotion. We can see how misunderstanding starts and swarms and explodes.

"I would rather head out into cobra country than spend one more minute with you!"

Then, in the dark, the person realizes, *Dammit. I'm in cobra country!* Back they go to make up with the person with the machete and the fire.

I watch, and I reflect on my own life, my own blind spots, the way fear makes me run naked into jungles like a maniac rather than working with those around me.

In my meditation, I have happened upon fear, endless fear. Fear of wasting time, fear of wasting a life, fear of not doing enough. I find a fear of not being special, not being first, not being unique. So much of my identity has been wrapped up in the ways I have protected myself from feeling fear that it didn't occur to me it was something I could let go. Clem should be important, right? If she's not important, then she's failed, right?

When we do the work and happen upon these huge beliefs that have defined us, it can be shocking that it has never occurred to us we could be another way. I ask myself, what would it be like to just be? Without any need to excel or succeed or be the best? What would it be like to find the joy in just being? If I never stand out, living each moment to its potential without ever making a mark, what would that be like? Why do I need to be first?

We judge success to further some outside structure: capitalism, economics, social rank, the judgment of society. What happens when we question structures that seem so fixed?

We are always looking for our reflection in these structures and in those outside ourselves to give us worth. I must be a great drummer in the field of drummers. I must be known as a better writer than most, or draw more people to my social media, or have the happiest demeanor, or know the most about a subject, or have the cutest dog, or the best relationship . . .

All these things are a reflection of judgments outside me. I ask myself, *Who says?* and everything changes.

What if I say: today my playing is a delight in the communal experience that is music. I have something to write because there is something I would like to say, and my joy in language is for its own sake. My heart is full for this pug splayed out and snoring. I am drawn to write these words not because I know anything, but because it seems to be what I am called to do at 10:35 on a Monday morning. Nothing I say is new or special, except in that it is my expression of being, right now. My whole life is an expression of my being.

I Am. In an hour, if I'm lucky, I may still be, finding another expression that rings true.

It feels like flying to let go of identity structures without fear. I see how much of life is based in fear, the fear propping up my creation. Fear of being seen as weak, as not special, as not the best, the happiest, the one who knows it all.

One small injury to identity and we are set down a path of misery, clawing our way back to prop up that structure so the reflection rights itself. I will work triple hard to make sure everyone knows I work hardest. If I am not constantly striving to meet the eyes of judgment and succeeding, then I am worthless and lost.

When we experience a blow to our identity, the fear is that we will disappear. Who am I if I am not the best? For all my life that has been how I have made sure I am fully here, to be striving. Who am I if I don't live up to that which has been deemed success?

When we really let go of ego attachment, when we release the fear, here we find ourselves, strong, invincible. This is who we are, with truth as ultimate support.

We get injured, and what rises is stronger and more reliable than on what we have depended before.

We must be the most beautiful we can be at all times, until we are on TV with the world watching, our naked body riddled with bug bites and dirt and pus. It has all been a facade. We say our strength is unexcelled until we haven't eaten for eight days and sit sobbing in the mud. Who is it who walks the six miles through jungle, starving, broken, delirious? Not that self who was afraid to break, afraid to let down the pretense of identity and step over the snake, swim past the crocodile. Your own soft, vulnerable body is just another scrambling animal getting to a goal.

Truth, strength, resilience, beauty. They are not what we have been told. When the survivors of the show get back to their normal lives, a newfound vulnerability is apparent. They seem softer, not harder, for having exhibited such feats of strength.

Our hearts crack open when we face down our fears, and our endless capacity for love shines clearest. I am so happy the work I do to let go of fear doesn't involve parasites and anacondas. Sometimes though, it feels no less dire.

73 I love a band.

I love being one of a small group forging a way through the landscape, experiencing days and nights together. The intangible connection outsiders intuit. The mystery of the moment after everything has been loaded and the van door shuts and what happens as we drive away. I love the animal protection that forms in a band, and the secret language that develops.

The language of music connects us in an intimate way. Buzz Osborne from the Melvins, when asked how to keep a band together for so long, said, "Find a common enemy."

It works. The soundman is condescending, the promoter weasels out of his promises, an offensive email hurts someone's feelings, a nine-hour drive puts everyone on edge. Whatever it is we fight, we fight together. Onstage, the musical communication rarely fails to smooth it over. The band vents its frustration in song and comes together yet again. The performance proclaims the unity.

I have been in great bands in my life. With one of them, we truly did forge our way across landscapes. I learned in that band the limits of what can hold together and what breaks apart.

What else has being in bands taught me? Communication, and how speaking from truth and with love can ease even the most difficult message. Being so close with others, traveling and working and creating, has made me more compassionate. Getting so close, you can't help but see how each person fights their own battles, just like you.

Being in bands has taught me how to truly give myself to joy of connection, gratitude for being able to count on others. Even through complicated webs of personality and difficulty, a common love for this path keeps us lightened and functioning.

I look at all the bands in my life and the lessons I learn. The band of family, how they teach me unconditional love: how to accept it, how to live it. The musical bands and their lessons of communication and cooperation. The bands of my friends and their lessons of openheartedness and kindness and fun.

There is the band of neighbors, whose dogs know my dog and with whom I chat or nod to as I rush through my days. The band of San Franciscans: maybe their lesson to me is how to monitor my road rage and to manage frustration at the flaunting of inequity. The band of Californians, with all our Hotel California dreams of what could be and of what was. The band of Americans, coming together as the ground moves under our feet, and we are forced to further define our union. The band of human beings and the lesson of the great gift of this life. The band of planetary beings and the symbiosis of working with all species for the benefit of all.

It is just physics, in a way. The small group is an expression of the whole. We look at particles and they are universes beneath our vision, reflecting the mirror of sky we gaze up to see. The universe is a hologram, each part containing the whole.

We are real, but not in the way we believe. We are energy, not matter, and the energy can't help but connect with every other energy body with which we interact.

In the van, traveling and laughing and connecting through the complications of matter and separateness, the lesson seems to be the same as at every other level: we are One. We are a bubble of energy traveling down a hologram of reality reflecting an illusion of thought.

I will be with the band again. We will play music and drive and laugh, and when the door of the van shuts, it'll be us against the world for a little while. Onstage, I will close my eyes and feel the connection, spread it out, expand the energy of the drums into the audience, above the venue, across the landscape, my energy traveling across the hologram of planet.

The borders I feel between myself and others drop away. What would it be like to live openheartedly, without the barrier of ego and the illusion of solidity? What would it be like to have as my purpose to recognize the same simple song, singing in the hearts of all?

I was walking the dog down the street after rising from meditation, open and neutral.

A man walked toward me at the far end of the block, screaming at someone or something, a barrage of violent curses. He was obviously mentally ill, yet from the minute my attention went to him I felt peaceful. I held him in my heart as he came down the block screaming. In this place of truth, I intuited there was nothing to fear.

Everyone on the sidewalk rushed to get away from him, and I kept strolling, letting the dog sniff about and stop where he wanted. The man came closer. I could see his ragged clothing, his face reddened by exposure, his body tensed with anger, yet I observed from this openness it didn't feel like anger driving him. His actions felt involuntary. I could intuit calm at the bottom of his outburst.

He got about ten feet in front of me, yelling all the way, and then his body relaxed. He looked me in the eyes and said, "How are you doing?"

"Oh, I'm doing all right."

"Is that a pug?"

"Yep, that's Henry."

"He looks like a fat little pug."

"Yeah, well, food is pretty important to him. Take care."

He walked past me, calmly, easily. Then, ten feet behind me, he commenced screaming at the world.

I see how this story could illustrate my descent into nihilism, as I put my life in the face of a potentially dangerous person without the proper self-preservation instinct. However, at all times I was aware, trusting that I was seeing the situation clearly, still prepared to grab the dog and run, should awareness tell me to do that.

More than anything, what I felt was trust. This man and I were no different in those moments he was barreling down the street. I felt open and ready to give him what he needed, there for what was required of me. If he had asked for money, or help, or needed to hurt me for some reason, my response would have come from truth, and I would have trusted the response. I would have given him what was in my pocket, crossed the street, protected the dog, whatever reaction was required. I guess he just wanted to have a relaxed conversation for a moment. As we spoke, love radiated from the compassion field.

It is not for me to know if this was the best action, but in those moments, it was unquestionably right. Maybe I was there to give him a moment of nonreactive calm.

Without reaction, without preference or judgment, one is in compassion. When there is no reactivity, then response comes as it should—from energy, not impulse.

What is interesting is how much easier it is to be compassionate to others than it is to oneself. Onstage, when I stumble out of the moment, what I hear is a berating voice warning of upcoming potential disasters, or negative thoughts of defeat.

That voice might always be there. These patterns of thought, though painful, are comfortable and familiar, and I seemingly can't do anything to stop them. I can stop listening though. In this sea of compassion, all attachment dissolves. I will play well, and I will screw up. I will watch fear and shame. I will live as I will live. I will act as I am to act, and from this place, it is.

75 Physicist Brian Greene was speaking about the Higgs boson and how reality is created from pressure, from interaction:

. . . The universe may be filled with an invisible substance called the Higgs Field, and as particles try to burrow through this environment, they feel a kind of resistance, which is where their heft, or their mass comes from. But we have to accept this strange idea that there is this invisible substance that is all around us.

. . . So, mass comes from an interaction. Exactly right. It's not something that is just sort of imbued from the get-go, or from the outside. Now, a parable that gives us some sense of how you can take that very strange story and make it seem less strange is to just think of fish in the ocean, or fish in a fish tank. Right there, swimming around, and they're really not aware that there is a part of the universe that's not filled with this watery substance. In fact, this water is so familiar to them that that is emptiness, that is their universe.

So there you have some beings that are living within an environment that is suffused with essentially an invisible something, water, and yet, because they're in it all the time, they don't know it. We are in the Higgs field all the time, we experience our interaction with it all the time, and that's why we don't even know it.[15]

Our reality is created from force, positive against negative. If the positive exists because of the pressure the negative is applying, then what is negative, really? Doesn't that make it positive, if its opposition to positive is what allows positive to exist?

I was rolling these things around in my head, and I had a dream. In my dream, I was thinking about this pressure, this force holding everything together and bringing reality into existence. Then, I started to be able to see right into the place where everything meets, the exact line where the force is applied. I was looking at people and things and could see a physical line dividing each one down the middle, where the positive and negative forces met. I kept looking closer and closer and suddenly realized that right there, in that place where reality was created, where energy becomes form, in that narrow space of pure pressure, there was no force and no pressure.

It was freedom I could feel in my whole being. It was a release, a nothing and an everything. It was as if at the center of all pressure and at the bottom of all reality was total freedom, total peace, devoid of any of this perceived force or battle or however I would describe reality.

In my dream, I opened my eyes and was overwhelmed with the beauty and vividness of the landscape around me. I was laughing, realizing that this had been all around me, this vibrant color, this gorgeous reality, and I had never really seen it. I was zooming around brilliant emerald mountains with flowers all over them, and I had never seen such color. I had never felt so free. I woke up joyful.

What is this reality, really? This force of the past pressing in on the present and future, bringing into existence this ego with emotion and thought, creating this edifice I call Clementine, which is continually created and holds itself together with the pressure of concept. Who is telling the story? What happens when I let go of all stories?

My ego tells me, if you let go of these things, this Clementine, the story of Clementine, you will die. In that expansive freedom, I ask myself: *Who is it who dies?* When I am in this light that continues and does not change, then death is yet another concept that blows away with the fog.

Maybe what dies is the belief that summer means anything other than the warmth on my skin and a cycle in flower beds. I choose freedom. At 2:00 p.m., the summer sky is a jewel of blue, a gift for whoever cares to see.

ROCK AND ROLL

76

"Rock and Roll." This fucking song. It taunted me for years and then suddenly allowed me to own it. I think I was running away from it, and it was running away from me. Somehow, we met.

For me, this song is about trying to unlearn a first impression. Expectation is a killer, and for years I expected to fail with this one. My impression from the start was that it was difficult. It is a difficult song to play. I can't get close to Bonham here. I have to adapt to my own limitations. I will admit I add more flash than competence. Shoot me.

Suddenly, though, I found the rock, the movement of the body that unlocks the swing. Playing the song became so much more simple from then on. The sound of the hi-hats here just about puts me in my grave, the ching ring like the swish of hips adding to the magic of sound. And John Paul Jones, for Chrissake. The guy is a master, could never be celebrated enough.

This song was on the top of many a setlist, for years, only to be kicked out on the climb to the stage, when we decided to start with "The Rover" instead. If I'm not feeling it, I'm not doing it.

The song was expendable until I stopped giving myself an out. *Work, motherfucker, or you're going to be miserable up there. Your choice.* Mind over limitation.

Playing this song is truly mind over matter until authority appears and the circle and stomp enters. Gotta keep it loose, or you're sunk. You must focus when this is the first song of the set, through any equipment snafus or unsteadiness in sound. Make sure you are rock solid. Focus right into the center of the strength you must embody to play this right, and keep that flame lit. Give yourself over to control, but let abandon carry you in.

You must have that swing going, that stomp. That is what gets the bodies moving. The energy of moving bodies propels the soundwaves until everything is one big wave. That's why three hundred–seat venues are the absolute best. We are all one pulse, and if I am playing the song right, we get to surf that truth.

77 Something has happened to Reno, Nevada. For years, I have known it as a dusty and desolate place. Last time I visited I found it thriving, with unique stores and diverse cuisine and new places going up. A crystal store, a real record store, a legendary guitar store, music venues and coffee shops and vegetarian restaurants.

Mainly though, it is the people who are remarkable. Kind and open and in love with their town. Several people had moved back to Reno recently after years away, and they were all so delighted with their decision. Folks seemed happy, easy. "The sky is like that every night," we were told proudly as we gaped at the sunset.

Now has Reno changed, or have I?

Our day was pretty perfect. The bass player had no delayed or cancelled flight for a change. The drive from San Francisco was traffic-free. My bandmates were in good spirits. The hotel was more comfortable than expected. Our dinner was tasty. The venue folks were delightful. The sunset looked like it was showing off. The band played as good as it has ever played, and the attendees were grateful. There was good bourbon. We got a late checkout from the hotel.

It has been over fifteen years of playing in Reno, and my impression has been of a colorless and run-down place. This was a different Reno. Was my impression fixed only because I had been unable to appreciate things for the last fifteen years? Would I have been able to recognize Reno's beauty back then?

In my life as a musician, I have played in all states but one. I have often been fascinated by what makes up my impression of a town.

Traveling in Europe, the band had a show in Croatia. We drove into town in a rainstorm. The roads were in bad shape, the buildings industrial and unlovely, and the venue was basically a warehouse by the train tracks. The promised meal was inedible, and I remember concrete and black walls and cold wind whipping into the room from the door.

We stayed in an Eastern Block high-rise that reminded me of the housing projects on the Lower East Side in New York City. One room, mattresses on the floor. The apartment was so small that the promoter of the show and his friends sat up all night at the kitchen table as we slept in the only other room. Did I mention I was playing in a metal band, and in 2002 this is what passed in Zagreb as a good gig?

We woke in the morning, piled into some cars, and were led to town. As we drove, the sun found its way out of the clouds. By the time we arrived at the patio of the breakfast place, the morning had become beautiful. We were seated in an area next to a peaceful waterway, the architecture stunning. Somehow, we found ourselves in the middle of a music box. People we encountered were smart and funny and gracious, the breakfast delicious, and when I unpacked my equipment the next night, I saw that someone had written "Zagreb Loves You" on my kick pedal case (which of course, I still have).

My impression of Zagreb? One of my favorite places. The Zagreb in my mind is now both of light and dark, but mostly, I remember the hard-working promoter and people who made sure our impression was not limited. In seeing the beauty of the place, I see the beauty of it all, the kind people who forsook their comfort for ours, the folks who forged a venue out of nothing because music was that important, and their insistence we see Zagreb in its best light, with laughter and coffee on a sunny day.

If I had only experienced that first night, I would say Zagreb was dark and gritty, my judgment of the whole country colored by this brief grimy night.

I have had many experiences like this. I have pulled into towns that seem to have not one redeeming or beautiful quality, and by the next morning I am wishing for more time. It is the people who change my view. If I can get over all my judgments about what I expect the place to be and see it for what it truly is, often through the eyes of a local, there is beauty in every place.

78   After the first night of a three-night run, I could feel myself comparing everything to the perfect day before. I watched my mind as I played the drums: *Last night, I played that fill better. Tonight is not going to be as good. Which makes sense since you can't have it so easy all the time. It was better last night, it sounded better last night, I played better, the girls played better . . .*

I watched these judgments take hold of my mind. Things were harder, not in the flow. I sensed I was doing this to myself, making the whole thing more difficult because it wasn't the same as the previous night's experience.

I felt physically tired. Altitude, my nemesis. I was doing what I always do when I feel tired, which is to overcompensate and speed everything up. I looked sheepishly at Gretchen, and she pantomimed falling backward, begging me to slow down. I settled down for about a song and then drifted away again, into speed land. I could tell she was having sound issues. The guitar cut in and out, an electricity issue. It was the first night on a new sound system in the venue. My snare head was new and not ringing out for some reason, and my crash cymbal decided to screw with me all night.

Was this just the way it goes, that the second night is always more difficult? Or is the second night always more difficult simply because of judgment, expectation, the idea it will not go as well as the night before?

Once we see the world from atop the mountain, once we see each person as the same as us, once we see all things as a divine expression, once we begin to realize true vibration and see all things as one, the problem we have as humans is that it seems necessary for us to go back down the mountain and make sure all the old ways of seeing things are still in place. We need to experience things as we have always known them, even if we've had a vision of a higher way. We don't think it is possible to stay up there. We expect for it all to come crashing down, the crashing instigated by this comparison to what we have known.[16]

I have a difficult day, so I assume the whole landscape is difficult. I have a perfect day, and the next day I assume I must trudge down the mountain to find fault in everything that happens, because yesterday was an anomaly and things can't possibly stay in such a flow.

Apparently, Clem believes beauty is fleeting, that a beautiful day is only able to occur once in a while. I see I have always expected flow states to eventually get blocked up, to not last. I have bought into the idea that the world kind of sucks, and the good things are these rare aberrations. I believe the top of the mountain is unattainable for good, and I am meant to be stuck forever wishing myself up to the top.

I have come to understand I can stop believing this.

If I take each moment and set aside any comparison or judgment and experience the now, what happens? I feel free. I see thought at a distance, and each thought is a judgment, or comparison, or expectation. It was shocking to me when I first did this. Each thought is a judgment!

If I arrive in a town and experience each moment with no need to compare or judge or expect it to be different, what is reality like then? Challenges may rise, but I might see each challenge as a way to learn how to stay in neutrality. Can I open my heart to each situation as it comes? What happens if my vision stays at a higher vantage point, seeing each person, each situation, each object in high esteem, as divine? What happens if I believe each difficult challenge in my life has been set here, by me, from which to learn?

My favorite existential question: What is reality? Are we creating it as we go? I seem to gain agency over my life when I decide to let go of the past and my history and the judgments created by history. Right now, how do I feel? What do I see? What if my heart remains open without some specter of the past demanding it remain guarded?

79 I checked in and sat at a bar near my gate. A young man sat next to me and on his forearm was a tattoo that said Be Here Now. We spoke about his trip to New Zealand and the enlightenment of travel. I let him know about Ram Dass and the book *Be Here Now*, which, funny enough, he didn't know about. He was happy to get the information. I got happy thinking of him reading Be Here Now for the first time.

I received a phone call from my singer. She was being taken to the emergency room with a serious illness.

For a moment, I got lost in dread and stress. Worried for my friend and her health. Worried about having to cancel the shows and the dread of inflicting stress on the venues and promoters. Anxious about the reputation of my band and business and the pain of having to tell my booking agent about all her lost work. Heartbroken for the people who had been looking forward to our rare visit to these areas. The ego panicked for a short time and my brain spun around and prevented any coherent thought.

Then, I took a breath and remembered. *Be Here Now.* My whole day, my whole life, has been pointing to this moment. Here, a wave of pain. Here, underneath, peace.

I saw Gretchen come walking across the white tile floor of the airport, and just the sight of her made me feel better. I felt all those waves of pain, waves of anxiety and stress, wash out of me as I looked at her. A feeling of peacefulness rose, the peace required when living through the ups and downs of a music career. The subtext of peace in the words "it's only rock and roll."

We made phone calls, cancelled flights, miraculously retrieved our bags, sat together in a quiet part of baggage claim, made sure all the ends were tied up. Then, we rolled the guitar and pedal board and cymbals and merchandise and suitcases upstairs and stood on the busy sidewalk, a little dazed, waiting for cars to take us to an unheard-of weekend in which we had nothing whatsoever planned.

I sat in evening rush-hour traffic and fell into Now. Happily, my driver was Brazilian, and I got to speak my crappy Portuguese with him. We spoke of feijoada and caipirinhas, and I showed him the photos of my epic visit to Brazil a few years past. We had a happy drive.

I heard from my singer. She was resting comfortably. The pug was ecstatic I was home and attached himself to me as I got on the couch. The Old Man had dinner waiting and found a Tom Petty documentary for us to watch. I found stillness at the base of it all.

For the first time in the history of the band, we needed to find a substitute for Gretchen for one show.

The substitute guitarist, Nili Brosh, had learned the songs in a month, which was remarkable in itself, since the music is known for its rather surprising arrangements, defined and deep feel, and technical chops. As soon as we started our practice the day before the show, I relaxed. The most important thing to me is that the feel is right, and she locked right in. Even in the first song, I could feel her easy intuition, and the connection between the drums and guitar was airtight. We were going to be in good hands.

Even though I had full confidence in the show musically, I was curious how the audience would accept this turn of events. I have been in female bands for close to thirty years, and there are few things I can count on. One of them is that any change throws people for a loop. Some other things:

The band and the players will always be underestimated. Underestimated for ability, for kindness, for humor.

People are much more familiar with us than they are with other bands. They feel free to hug us, to order us around, to lecture us on things of which they know very little, to tell us intimate details about their health and relationships, to write and ask that we call to talk to them. A woman wrote to tell us that her forty-three-year-old son decided he no longer wanted to be a virgin after seeing our videos, could they have backstage passes?

If those who underestimate our senses of humor could see our reactions in these moments, there would be no question that we can take a joke.

Compassion is big with us, so it takes a lot to offend. People will tell me what to think, how to think, and wrongly correct me. They will tell me I have gotten fat, as if I need someone to alert me to any weight gain, then in the next breath tell me they like me best of everyone in the band. They will somehow believe that I want to hear them tear down my bandmates when I get offstage, while I am still sweaty from sharing a beautiful two-hour intuitive musical ecstasy with those bandmates.

The other thing I have learned is that at some point, people will assume we are all secretly plotting against each other and all other female musicians. I don't wonder where this comes from. The female catfight is a whole reality-TV industry unto itself. When men create the culture, they create the narrative of women fighting for their attention: this is Feminist Theory 101. Again, in the circle of the band, this perspective is often funny and puzzling and tiring.

The examples popular culture dish out are not the way real people live their lives. We are all pretty aware of that and becoming more aware of it daily. Our stereotypes dissolve when we interact, when we open our hearts and see into everyone's personal struggles to belong. When we take control of how we see reality, the truth can be dazzling. Turn off all media for a few days, take a lot of walks, interact with some strangers, and see for yourself.

The night of the show, what I was expecting didn't happen. I got offstage and rather than being inundated with comparisons of the two guitarists, it was a celebration of the differences. "Two degrees of awesome." This was the consensus. The two guitarists are different players, different sensibilities, different histories that both connect them and create two unique ways of interpreting the songs. It was a different show. Different and good, different and fun, different and entertaining. I was proud of the audience.

Music is the conduit through which I access love. We each have access. In each note played, in each clear regard of another, we see the universe. No matter what silliness is causing paroxysms of laughter in the backstage room.

The big trees are boxing on the hill. I hear a dove that sounds like a whippoorwill. The pine leans to whisper to the eucalyptus, and these great gossiping giants oversee the park's expanse of green. Parrots and bumblebees. Pairs of woodpeckers. I am fortunate my appreciation of beauty has deepened at a time when I live in this landscape. I get dumbstruck at this act of fortune as I lie in the park with the pug.

The thing I adore about the pug is that he too appreciates the beauty of it all. He finishes his treat off first thing, then sets to rolling, setting aside dignity in a committed free-for-all, with legs akimbo and a great deal of snorting delight. Then, as if nothing out of order just happened, he sphinx's out in the shade, with his eyes cracked and his nose in love with the air.

The pug is pretty great at reminding me to be right here. I watch as a young woman speeds through the park, talking on her phone. Her cute dog is leaping on her, leaping on the bench, vying for her attention. *We are in the park!* he seems to say. *Sit down, take a breath. Trees!*

The pug chose correctly when he chose me. I flip over and watch a hummingbird frolic in the dark fir tree, and the pug takes another roll-around. I imagine myself up there, the city laid out below with its own magic, and the sweet ocean air tossing me about. If I were the hummingbird, I would never come down.

There is an astrological term called the Saturn Return. This says that at the twenty-seventh year, the whole planetary cycle starts over for us, and we go through a new birth. When I was entering my twenty-seventh year, I went to see a legendary psychic. She told me, *The next three years will be particularly difficult for you. Things you no longer need will fall away in shocking ways. You will question everything you know and everything you are. The way out? Pick one thing, it doesn't matter what it is. Do that thing every day. You will ask yourself, "Why am I doing this?" Just remember what I'm telling you, just do it. That will bring you to where you should be.*

You probably can guess the thing I picked was drums. I really did question what I was doing, just as she said.

I was not present in the same way then. I was in a state of mental and emotional turmoil much of the time. I notice that I am different now, and it makes me feel happy. I can experience struggle and never get worked up. Life is different now. I note it.

Then, I let go.

The past is a window through which we see the present. I want to step out of that window and truly be right here, without the color of anything past keeping me from the Now. If I am not comparing this moment to any that has come before, then I am pure experience.

It feels frightening to say that. If we don't know the past, then we will repeat it. We have heard it again and again.

No matter how much care I take, things go terribly wrong in some moments. Houses burn, tragedy happens, and beyond the big things are all these myriad stresses and problems. If I don't remember the past, how can I work to avoid these things?

The answer: I can't. We learn as we go. We make decisions that seem innate, but if we are truly in the present moment, we make decisions from a field of truth, not the past. I don't need to remember burning my finger to know not to put my finger on a stovetop. If I am truly present, I will burn my finger or not burn my finger depending on the truth of the moment. Maybe burning my finger is a lesson I am to learn. My finger will hurt, yet I will remain in the field of neutrality, allowing the experience as it unfolds.

We think of that neutral field as a kind of zombie-like state, with no feeling, but it is exactly the opposite. We feel every joy and anxiety fully, and yet neutrality comes with allowing these things to pass through without getting caught on them, without inviting them to stay and ruin the day. This is the glory of living, of being present for your moments.

The more we live from this state, more and more subtle nuances of beauty rise and are felt. The heart opens, and love beats exquisitely.

WHOLE LOTTA LOVE

83 "Whole Lotta Love" is the song I have played the most of any Led Zeppelin song and never the same way twice.

To improvise onstage is a complete riot, and this song has a very long part into which improvisation drops in and out. To improvise, you must zoom out in order to find that spot in which all four voices are equally heard and conversing. Imagine each voice in a corner before you, with the drums in one corner. You must follow the conversations happening between the four corners while creating a melody that sings beneath it all and plays in the repartee. Images must rise and fall and paint your musical picture. Ideally, you play a rhythm that is hypnotic for a while, then froth it up to get a bit sweaty.

In this part of the song, everyone gets a moment in the sun, each instrument their time to shine a little firework. We culminate in an all-hands-on-deck climax. When it works, it works.

A great benefit of playing in a band like this is you get the education and influence of playing John Bonham's parts, but the songs have moments built in for a recess of castle building and free play. When everything's working and the sound system is with us, we can start a real hula hoop of energy crashing around the perimeter.

Within the structure of Bonham, I get to understand who I am as a drummer. Within the rhythm of drumbeats, I find melodies and abilities that are all mine.

I always loved writing in a structure. I think of the sonnets I wrote in high school and how the rigid form allowed me freedom to dream deeper into each image. John Bonham's parts are an engine in which I spin. When writing lyrics, the gift of the framework of rhythm seems to spur the consonants and all that follows.

A great love in my life is songwriting. It feels so natural, and somehow, being a drummer taught me how to write a song.

I start by creating an electronic drumbeat, then place live drums alongside the drumbeat, then allow the words to rise from the harmony of those two rhythmic voices. Lyrics are a puzzle divinely inspired. Pure expression can happen when singing your own words.

Seeing a song move from Clem mind to manifestation onstage is a thrill of thrills. I sing a song a thousand times before it goes before people, and when I am on that stage it feels like the first time every time.

Within the drum is a voice.

Stories are right there.

My first show playing drums was on the West Side of Manhattan. It was in a little neighborhood I don't know the name of anymore, between Chelsea and the West Village, a block from the West Side Highway. I remember walking around the sidewalk with my friend Elizabeth before the show in a state of terror, saying, *What the hell am I doing? I was never going to be a musician!*

After that first show, I never again was scared before I got onstage behind the drums. I was always a ham as a kid, performed at every opportunity. Behind the drums, I get to be even more comfortable. There is a bunch of wood and metal and other people between me and the audience. Maybe I get a little more focused when I play very big places, because I realize that over, say, the Warfield Theater sound system, any kick drum errors are going to be really amplified, but that is not fear. More like challenge. When I am behind the drum kit, I feel more confident and comfortable than almost anywhere else. I take it as a sign I found my instrument.

After not writing lyrics in years, I was sitting for days in a hospital room with my recovering mother, and an album of songs poured out. I brought them to the band, and Anna sang them. It was spectacular to have such an amazing singer sing my words.

After that record, it started to press down on me: *I think I need to sing my lyrics.* I wrote more songs. Took more voice lessons. Wrote a record and figured out how to create sounds and arrangements in the computer. Recorded the record. Put a band together. Booked a show.

Enter fear. Here I was, in the same place I had been twenty years earlier, walking around the block shaking, trying to make sense of finding myself on a detour when I didn't remember turning off the road. *I was never going to be a singer!*

All the baggage of a lifetime of unsuccessful singing performances, all the uneven confidence, all the uncertainty, the judgment and public opinion—welcome to the front of stage.

Suddenly, I found myself pushed into stage fright. Before I would get up, my body would shake uncontrollably. I would start to panic and look to my writing partner, Justin Caucutt, taking some comfort in his wry smile and his, "You're going to be fine!"

Onstage, I would sort of black out. When I would later remember things I had said between songs, I would be completely humiliated. I announced to the audience that I felt the whole experience was brutal. I held a plastic water bottle during the entire heartfelt ballad. For some reason, I just could not get ahold of myself. For some reason, I wanted to keep doing it.

I love to sing. I love to tell a story in lyric. I love to perform a song and experience that place when the listeners connect and there is a still silent attention that bonds us all in the moment. I can now say I have something to say.

I figured out that a lot of stage fright is about not feeling prepared enough, so I worked hard on freeing myself from constricting insecurities. When I get onstage I think, *Well, I will just do what I do.* It is the same mindset I relied on when I started performing on drums. I aim for freedom, while present and connected to the audience the way a front person should be.

There is a kind of deep listening required, a way of paying attention from the center of myself so I can truly hear what is being said while being able to speak my own story.

Maybe what I have been listening to this whole time is my own voice and not the song. Maybe what I have been hearing as I stand onstage and sing is the voice in my head and all the voices in the river of thought that pull me out of the moment. What would happen if I listened to the whole song as it's being played and just sing what I would most want to hear? What if the song sings me?

It makes me think. Maybe when I was changing course midstream all those years ago what I was doing was listening, unknowingly, with an ear to that voice underneath the fear, underneath the questioning, to the voice that knew all along what the right path would be.

It seems like every time I stop midway along the drive from Seattle to San Francisco after a weekend of shows, "Here Comes the Sun" plays in the hotel restaurant.

I drop off the band for morning flights and drive seven or eight hours until about 5:00 p.m. Then, a stop in Oregon. I always pick a hotel with a restaurant. This time I lucked out on a last-minute booking at a hotel with a hot tub in the room. Badass.

I have several germophobic friends who eschew any hotel room bathing, but I choose to trust that people generally do their jobs well and thoughtfully and give the enamel a good scrubbing between travel-worn bodies. I don't have a good bathtub at home, so any opportunity for hot bubbly water, I'm in. After a weekend of four shows, hot stages, lots of driving, and goofy sleep, there was no way I wasn't getting in that tub.

I used to drive the fourteen hours straight through. The Old Man has taken truck with that, concerned for my safety, so to keep the peace I now stop midway. It is a forced vacation I look forward to. I catch up with a few dear friends on the drives, listen to podcasts or audiobooks, gaze at the gorgeous landscapes. Time goes too quickly.

I have known few people who enjoy driving as much as I do. My father was a truck driver when I was born, and I guess the love of the road sank into my bones. I am prideful of nothing as much as my driving. I have accomplished legendary (in my own mind) drives: Dallas to San Francisco in less than a day, Boston to San Francisco in three days. It may be that I decided to be a musician just so I would have an excuse to drive.

People dislike driving because they focus on the destination and not on the meditative journey. My mind swings wide open as the landscape rolls by. I watch the birds, the hawks and the little flocks that fly alongside the bushes. This time I saw an eagle, in a nest at the top of a telephone pole.

In motion, the stable life is up for examination, a gift to see from a distance. People focus too much on driving as a way to arrive. When the focus is purely on the destination, the stress of anticipation makes for no fun. I will save pointing out parallels to the way we live our lives. Humanity seems to be becoming aware of how quickly life goes when all you do is rush toward the end.

The hot tub happened, for longer than I care to admit. I watched a documentary on my laptop. Then a rest, then dinner. The restaurant was homey, and as it was Monday night of a holiday weekend, there were only a handful of tables occupied. A man played a guitar and sang, and his voice sounded like James Taylor. *"It seems like years since it's been here."* What is it like to capture sunlight and turn it into song?

I sat at a table, ordered the vegetable pasta, wrote a train of thought on the hotel room receipt. Maybe at one point in my life it felt strange to sit alone in a restaurant, snuggled into a corner writing on napkins and oblivious to the room. If it was ever strange, that was a long time ago. I used to feel more conspicuous, but one of the marvelous things about aging is that you become invisible, and you realize no one pays attention to anything you do. Were they ever paying attention?

My body is all of which I am aware. I captain it like a raft in the center of an empty ocean. I am an unknown person in a random hotel that hugs a mountain range on a planet drifting among dark and stars.

As I was walking around the hotel grounds after dinner, I lifted into the solar system and saw myself from up there, a little light flashing on and off. A star, a shadow. Then I fell down, right into this body. My little vehicle.

I have let go of the feeling of being observed or needing to be observed. Anonymity is glorious.

Why did I ever think anyone was paying attention?

The documentary I watched in the hot tub was about Thomas Keating, a Catholic monk who connected Eastern thought and Christian doctrine in his teachings. My favorite part was when he said:

> *I was walking through the grove. It was dead quiet, with the lovely leaves in the summertime. All of the sudden, this breeze came up and all these trees just burst into action, shaking madly like this, more than any charismatic group you have ever seen. I had the feeling: this is a standing ovation! It felt like I was being greeted by all these wonderful leaves, and it wasn't just a few. The whole place was just exploding, leaves and branches, in glee. Then, fortunately, some degree of humility resurrected in me. I said, they're not waving at me, they're waving at God in me. So I waved back to the God in them.*[17]

We go from perspective to perspective. Younger, I thought everyone was watching, so my movements became narrowed and exacting lest they be judged. Older, I see I am invisible, my movement through the world like a fluttering moth in the span of time and space. This doesn't bother me, as everywhere I look, the God in me waves a joyful greeting to it all.

85 Alice Parker, "a composer, conductor, and teacher who's been shaping the universe of chorale music for most of her ninety years," said:

> *What we miss when we don't have song is the means of creating a community, of creating a whole out of a group of people. And it doesn't matter if it's a group of people in an old folks' home that can't really sing anymore, or if it's a kindergarten classroom, or a nursery school classroom, or a bunch of seventh-grade boys who can be fairly hard to get to function as a unit.*
>
> *Wherever they are, if you get them on a song, you can establish a kind of group feeling that is really—well, it's exemplified at its most marvelous after a perfectly wonderful concert when the last note is sound, and you get that silence in the room, which is a silence of completion, which is opposite from an anticipatory silence. But it just means that everyone—it's as if all of our inner ions have been scheduled to be moving in the same direction at the same time.*[18]

Inner ions all moving in one direction. I recognize our bodies as vibrations, as collections of small *kalapas*[19] that blink on and off constantly. Music affects us with waves of sound moving through these tiny particles, jostling them around, massaging them. I remember that long-ago meditation, in which I saw myself as a mass of tiny particles and watched as the sound of the rain moved through me, shaking and shimmering the little pieces that made me up.

Maybe that is what music is doing, pointing our particles in the same direction. It feels this way when I am playing certain shows.

The Miners Foundry in Nevada City sounds great. The high ceiling is made of wooden beams, the best kind of ceiling in any venue. It lifts away any harsh high frequencies and rounds and warms the whole tone.

I felt the ions in the room, all the kalapas vibrating together as the audience sang along with the songs. All the particles, all the sound waves, all the energy, the energy I call love.

Maybe this is the beauty of music, that it fills us and reminds us of this awareness beneath our barriers. The waves moving through you then move through me, wrapping and connecting us on a subatomic level. It certainly feels this way when we are together, moved by song. It certainly feels this way when we sing together, blending our voices.

Maybe the division and difficulty of the past years are here to spotlight this truth, that we are more connected than we believe. There is such power in raising our voices together. We vibrate as a whole, and our individual voices long to find a chorus of truth. Music communities formed of diverse people remind us of our connection.

When there are eight hundred people in a room, connected by music and vibrating on a deep level together, how easily our bodies are affected by other energies too. Energy of thought, energy of stress, of fear. How delicate our constitutions. How profoundly we are influenced by the frequencies of others. If those around me are in pain, how their pain must travel through me as well.

This is my duty then, to generate as much positive frequency as possible. To be empathetic to the fear and pain of those around me. To learn to release these things in myself only helps the whole. We move together toward a new vibrational field, one in which all voices sing together in power, in joy, in truth, in justice. My path is to find a way to feel my pain, transform it. I contribute to the field around me with energy and power. I want to bring us together, releasing suffering, uniting.

If there is no "I," if there is no "you," and instead we raise our voices in one harmony, is this truth? Can we believe that all our ions vibrate together? All the issues we fight over seem to dissolve when we are here, aware of this vibration of love that overcomes all division. We can raise our voices together. We are being challenged to find this one song.

Perhaps the dark times we are living through are a kind of birth: a great movement from individualism to awareness of connection. Perhaps we are being called to move our ions in one direction, pointed toward the injustice that keeps us from peace and happiness, that keeps us from the understanding that we are worthy of, and gifted with, limitless grace.

86

There is never much glamour in buildings that house monthly rehearsal studios, and this sense of grittiness is familiar to most musicians. There is a feeling of rolling up your sleeves and going to work as you drive by the docks and the wholesale warehouses and the taxi companies. Somewhere in the world, there are clean and shiny hourly rental studios that the big names use, but most of us practice in the low-rent areas of cities, diesel fumes coughing on us as we arrive.

The room is a decent size, but the amount of equipment closes in. I don't consider myself a gear-hound by any means, but still, I have more than I need. Three drum kits and bins of pieces and parts that served a purpose and may one day serve another.

The Old Man is a collector. There are two lofts in the room, and his loft is crammed with amps and guitars and gear. Really, mine is no better. It is necessary to store back catalog merchandise, CDs, and posters. The band has a full setup of stage lights, and that takes up room as well.

Basically, the room is crammed full.

I spent some time trying to make it feel more spacious. I hung muslin over the dusty black baffling to lighten it up and went overboard on fairy lights, my version of decorating. I gave away a big dumb BASS BEER mirror that was taking up space. I dusted and put down another rug.

The bands who practiced in the studio twenty-five years ago were punk rock animals, and the carpet is disgusting. I can't blame it all on them, but I like to. Spilled beer. Duct tape ground in. Loading gear through the grimy parking lot in the rain at four in the morning tracks in grime. We would do ourselves a favor to replace the carpet, but that would mean carting all that stuff out of there. The thought is too daunting.

When time is precious and so many things seem to take me away from the studio, if I am going to be there, I want to be working on music, not cleaning.

I close the door, and I step inside the light of creative mind. The beauty of that space for me is obviously not in the way it looks but in the silence and possibility. The drums are all mic'd up, and all I have to do is push a button to record. There are electronic interfaces in which I can get lost for hours. Sometimes, I play around with using a guitar to spark ideas, yet another toy in the creation wonderland.

In my university class on Virginia Woolf, *A Room of One's Own* was important to me. I resonated with a decision to fight for creative expression, even through years when I had no idea what that expression would be. I would not have imagined that my own room would look like this mess of chaos, but I love it all the same.

87 When we have a goal of a daily practice of anything, we run the risk of falling into a funk or negative self-talk when we miss a day. I see discipline as a balance of keeping it solid and light all at the same time. Doing our best, forgiving the slips.

During a month of touring, I thought a lot about this practice.

There is such a benefit of a daily meditation practice, however you see it. Our habit is to forget about that place of peace or equanimity we discover on the cushion. We sit and light the candle and ding the little bowl and find the center of breath. Then, we jump up and head into the day, and we get back into the mind. We get carried away by irritations and stresses and forget our time on the cushion as we rush through. Then, next morning, we again let it all go for ten minutes, twenty minutes, and then off we go again, rushing around. We forget to remember.

Those ten minutes do begin to sink in. We see it in small ways. Maybe we are not as quick to get frustrated in traffic, or maybe we listen a little longer to someone before jumping into anger. Maybe the day has a little more space in it, or we remember to appreciate the breath of afternoon breeze. Little by little, the discipline of a daily practice does begin to change us. We begin to access that ground of equanimity that is our true nature.

Driving is meditation too. The wide landscapes, the distraction of basic motor function, the hum and rumble of the vehicle on pavement, these things make for a mind state that is like the alertness of meditation. My practice while sitting on a cushion can be mimicked while driving, as it affords this same awareness with some version of quiet.

Can I stay in the heart as I set about to unload the van, set up the drums, sound check, speak about hospitality with the production manager, repark the empty vehicle, set up the merchandise, submit the guest list, say hello to early arrivers?

I continually check in and notice what is happening inside: a feeling of fatigue, a frustration, an annoyance, a pain, a puzzle, a connection. Problems arise, solutions appear. Where is equanimity in it all? Why does the grumpy stage manager rile me so? I watch myself act out and then feel regret for letting someone get to me, for letting compassion slip. I examine the Clem who thinks she has been injured, I feel the injury, and in feeling it, find that self who can never be injured. I smile. I find the heart connection. I let their problem be all theirs.

Or I grumble and stay angry until later, when I can really get underneath the challenge and find my way to generosity.

Around and around I go, day in and day out of a tour. Watching what arises, allowing Clem to go through what she is here to go through. I see how practice has now left the cushion and is a moment-to-moment exercise. How do I keep present, even if the way I am reacting is not a very "Zen" way to be? How is a spiritual path supposed to look, anyway?

88 The drives through a snowy winter in the North country are dazzling. There was chain control all along Donner Pass, so I looped down around Bakersfield and up through Vegas to get to Salt Lake. The drive from Vegas reminded me of the stunning landscapes of Sedona, with the striated rock and the delicate desert colors. The following days we drove to Idaho and then to Jackson Hole, through white-frosted mountains and Wedgwood-blue skies.

We traced a triangle, five hours on each leg, plenty of time to chat leisurely of idea and of memory. The vistas appealed to Gretchen's favored color palette, and I smiled as she fell in love with a mountain rising out of the snowy plains. The bass player was unimpressed by the snow, seeing it as a big jerk forcing everyone to stay inside. I delighted in her grumpiness about the cold. Holly is a Texas girl, through and through, and does not truck with this snowy baloney.

Anna, resting her voice, alternated between sharing in the conversation and snuggling into blankets to nap. Singers have it the worst when it comes to care between shows. Drummers keep in limber shape and try to get some sleep, guitarists and bassists warm up their hands, but singers have delicate vocal chords to tend, susceptible to fatigue, dehydration, dry air, cold air, overuse, tension. Anna never has a problem when she hits the stage, due to a combination of fortitude and care.

It's snowing lightly in the Badlands in South Dakota. We are between tourist seasons, and this weather does not make for a popular day for a park visit, so we rarely spot another car. Hiking is impossible when it's wet in the Badlands, since the combination of clay and volcanic ash makes for slippery pathways. We get the place to ourselves.

The snow on the rock formations calls forth shapes in stark 3D. The colors move between vibrant and monotone. Smell of sage and snow, layers of pinks and reds and white and green, rugged crevices and unreal staggering peaks. We drive from one observation point to the next and ooh and aah at the sights.

The park opens out into a long drive through the prairie. There is two percent of wild prairie left in the US, and this is most of it. The sky is gray and the clouds low, and a long wooden walkway leads into the grass. We slip and slide on the ice out and out and out, until we stand with the land undulating around us as if we are standing on top of an ocean. The sky seals up the edges of our sight. I hear only the sound of my heart, the breeze on my cheek, trickle of water, noises of small birds. There is no hum of humanity, no airplane or car noise.

Laura Ingalls Wilder is from a town nearby, and I imagine for a second that I too am living in the long-ago world of prairie that her books enchanted me with as a child. A thought comes through about how much writing I would get done if I lived then, middle of nowhere, but I can't hold on to that imaginary scenario long. I have a sense of the wind coming from the edges of the earth. I am aware only of expanse of mind, expanse of sky, the opening in my chest that seems to have become porous. For a moment, I am the sky, the plains, a stalk of wheat blown through with the wind of time.

It occurs to me just how different we are now and what is gone. I don't forget that living in a cabin on a prairie was probably challenging much of the time, with the fear of starvation and weather and illness and other people. How much of the time was spent in this wide awareness? What was it like to live from this place of union with sky and earth?

89 Indian paintbrush, bluebonnet, Texas star. I always wanted to be a writer who knew the names of flowers, so there you go. These names run incessantly through my mind as we wind though the hill country of West Texas, springtime green and splashed with color.

I find myself imagining that at the far reaches of my range of sight there is an ocean waiting with a blue promise. For all this beauty, I am not suited for landlock. The sky is so large I have spells of vertigo in which the air feels sucked out of me, as if the sky is pressing on my lungs and squashing me. Then, I recite the flowers: Indian paintbrush, bluebonnet, Texas star. I allow my eyes to fill with the color and the sky and the expanse of land that is laid out in rolling relief before me, and I breathe.

The last night of this leg of the tour is in Marfa, a town of artists and a breed of people who want to get away while being in the center of things at the same time. I meet an artist[20] who paints the light of the desert sky onto canvases, dazzling in her vision. I wonder if the sky is the reason so many are flocking to the town or if theirs is a desire to be in proximity to the rare people who can translate its song.

We go through Arizona and El Paso and West Texas and Austin, then backtrack this direction. As I drive through this expansive beauty, I can't help but think of the drama unfolding miles away at an arbitrary border, which spotlights the worst aspects of humanity: people fleeing their homes because of corruption and poverty, people defending an intangible state of being, people forgetting the value of life and demeaning others in cruel and inhuman ways.

The doves cry in the dry green bushes around the little cabins, and there is a fat horsefly who hovers near me, breaking the silence with his aggressive wing song. I spend some time rescuing the bees who have mistaken pool for sky. I can't stand to see them flapping wildly on the surface.

I sit on a patio as the last rays of the sun light the sky. Bats spin by, and small bird sounds break the stillness here and there. I hear laughing coming from the hot pool, and I'll go there soon to see what the fun is. I don't see many stars yet, but the moon is bright behind me. I can never tell what face people see there, the man in the moon. I always just see the moon, in all its shining glory.

I am thinking about the folks at the border, wondering if ever the refugees are able to rest in the cradle of the natural world as they make their journey, if ever the people defending the border recognize the natural magnificence they are trying hard to defend: Big Bend, transmutation of sky, smell of mesquite and the primeval mountains steady in their regard, and always, the promise of the blue sea beyond.

Indian paintbrush, bluebonnet, Texas star. I consider what has been lost and gained.

90

A heat wave surprises everyone, and my dreams of settling in to the breezy days of home give way to caring for an overheated pug. Henry is offended by rain, delighted by snow, angry at ice, and surprised by heat. When it's hot out, he looks at me with wide eyes, distressed at his labored breathing. I worry about him all day. He is in and out of the bathtub filled with cool water, as we try to recover from sleepless, sweaty nights of his ceaseless panting and my hallucinatory dreams.

It cools off. Finally, the park. We lie in the grass, half-sun/half-shade as we like to do, and the trees welcome us back with a flurry of leaves let loose by the dancing ocean air. There are parrots in the branches above, and now and then a rain of twigs and red berries fall on us and around us. We take it as a gift. Welcome home.

After all my travel, I discovered a new development in the back garden: a mockingbird seems to have taken up residence. I am not sure if the jays have been supplanted, but the endless singing is something we are getting used to. There is nothing else we can do. This guy is truly a virtuoso, and it seems as though his repertoire is never-ending. He is prolific, a Schubert, a Bach, or like Paul McCartney or Robert Plant, moving through genres and moods at whim.

I meditate in the living room, as the heat has made the back rooms unlivable. As soon as I sit—closing my eyes, breathing deeply, and opening to stillness—the bird starts up, fairly frantic, with a song so varied and quickly changing it seems pointedly disruptive. I watch annoyance rise up: *Can't you see I'm meditatin' here?!* I quickly see the futility and humor of denying birdsong in my experience of truth and being.

Later, I came upon this Mary Oliver poem:

> *This morning*
> *two mockingbirds*
> *in the green field*
> *were spinning and tossing*
>
> *the white ribbons*
> *of their songs*
> *into the air.*
> *I had nothing*
>
> *better to do*
> *than listen.* [21]

As I sat on my little cushion with the dog snoring nearby, I too had nothing better to do than listen. I moved into the song, getting closer and closer, until I was inside of it, watching and listening in a way that was almost like being in the middle of a symphony, with all its voices and colors and crescendos. The sound persisted until it was not sound and instead spread out like a scroll, a wave, carrying me further and further into a feeling of openness.

The meditation lasted an hour. When I finally rose and turned the kettle on, I realized the birdsong had suddenly stopped. As I sat on the couch to write, the air in the room fell silent. Even the refrigerator lumbered into stillness.

91 In a Shamanic journey I asked, *How can I help the world?*
What I heard was:

The world helps you. Let the world love you. Allow the world to love you. Allow the world to show you its beauty. Allow the world to show you its kindness, how much love. That's how you help the world. Allow yourself to be loved. You have to learn that you're able to be loved.

Allow the world to love you. Allow the world to sing your song. Allow yourself to open to the divine in all ways. Approach the world in this way. Question definitions of bad and good. Allow love to flow—it is the only answer to every question. Allow love to flow into action. Allow love to flow into thought. Allow love to flow into movement of the heart, the simplicity of the heart. Whenever there is a judgment or barrier or border, it is an illusion. There is such joy.

When the drum calls me back, the memory of the smell of the Vipassana meditation center in North Fork, California, hangs around me.

I often think of the early morning walk to the meditation hall and the faces of the single yellow daffodils lining the path up the hill.

In one of the retreats, I became fixated on the manzanita trees, their spindly dark red trunks, the light green color of the leaves, the pink hanging bouquets of flower. It is inevitable that the senses become more vibrant when meditating for ten hours a day. The contrasting colors of the manzanita were almost too much to bear.

I fantasized about having a garden of manzanita one day, how it would be to set out a picnic among such a gorgeous color combination. I wanted to wrap myself in these colors and shapes.

I guess, really, I was longing to be a bird.

Since then, I have tried with limited success to see manzanita trees in the same way. Maybe I haven't come across them at that exact time of their blooming. Maybe the trees at the retreat center are extra beautiful because of the energy of the thousands of meditators passing by, hearts opening to the field of love vibration on which all reality sits. Maybe this kind of energetic food makes the trunks a little redder, the green of the leaves more arresting, shocking against the red.

In *The Shaman Within,* Claude Poncelet writes of Shamanic practices that entail traveling to the spirit of a tree, or a rock, or the ocean, and becoming this being. He merged with a mountain, to understand what the mountain had to teach: "I felt the wind upon my sides. I felt deep compassion for all creatures and beings living upon me—trees, bushes, mammals, birds, snakes, insects, humans. I felt love, and I cared for all. I knew I was being taught being, becoming, and compassion and that these qualities were somehow being imprinted in me. I retransformed very slowly and thanked the mountain. I felt peaceful and connected, part of the One."[22]

Driving to Sacramento from San Francisco, I once came through the high yellow hills into the strip malls heading into Vacaville, and I was suddenly startled by the personality of a low green hill a little way back from the highway.

I hadn't been noticing the natural world as I drove, and the hill shocked me, as if somehow calling for my attention. It was joyful and perky, that hill. Behind this web of traffic and asphalt and commerce was this gorgeous, squat little being, just happy to be recognized.

Communicating with our natural world seems more and more important as we move forward. With each modern natural disaster, it is as if our society keeps being shocked as nature draws attention to itself. I think of that little hill, huddled in noise and grime and yet transmitting joy. *I'm here if you want to take a look! Just hanging out loving you!*

I think of those manzanita trees on that beautiful land, a property devoted to providing space and time for people to freely connect with the truth of being. We are connected, those trees. Having communed deeply once, so forever. I imagine my love for them infusing their branches, protecting them from forest fires, and from the thoughtlessness of humanity's forgetfulness.

ACHILLES LAST STAND

When I started the band, a friend who had been drumming for twice as long as me said, "I'll tell you something. 'Achilles Last Stand.' Don't even try it. It'll just bum you out."

This admonition has hung with me from the start, that this song will always be beyond me. I am not fighting that opinion too hard, since that is what a goodly percentage of my self-awareness has to say: don't even try. I try. It gets closer to me, that glorious gallop. I think we will dance one day, Achilles and me.

I will embrace fearlessness.

There is a fearlessness in Alan Watts that is high art. He saw the value in recognizing that physical manifestation is an important aspect of realization. To have been a self-proclaimed sensualist in the late 1940s and 1950s was to embody a texture of experience beyond my own, and gives me the feeling of the German word *fernweh*, the longing for places never been (also called *farsickness*).

I would add "time" to the longing. Times and places, long ago and far away. The ache of desire to have lived Watts's incarnation is the feeling of lounging on a velvet couch in a tapestried room in Big Sur, 1950, with Henry Miller, Joseph Campbell, a female shaman, Anais Nin, and Aldous Huxley at the dinner table. Good grief, there is an almost sensate longing to have lived these stories. That is certainly something to investigate in my next meditation, that longing to have lived someone else's life.

Maybe what I should do is find the exact energy I feel in this vision of the past and see if I can bring that energy to me in the present.

Well, I dearly love stories, for all my work in making sure they don't take hold of me. To put myself in those places, to feel atmospheres, to imagine the light of the strong energetic fields of those great minds mingling about—it is delicious. Alan Watts and his crew and a dinner party. I can't imagine somewhere I would more like to be.

Some of that stuff folks were into around that time, like the naked therapy sessions, I balk at, but who cares, bring it on. So much of the opening taking place in the early 1950s was on the heels of the louche and tense end of the '40s, and taking place in the hearts of those educated classically, at least for the British. It seemed to be a floodgate that opened first in the intellectual community, then roared to suburbia in the 1960s.

The influence of Eastern spiritual thought is a key here. Ramana Maharshi was still in the world, and Krishnamurti, and Neem Karoli Baba. Yogananda's visit to America in the 1920s was a faucet turned on, and in the 1950s the interest in the East moved like a deluge through university departments and the religious and literary worlds. According to Alan Watts:

> *Such people have in mind an idealized vision of the mystic as a person wholly free from fear and attachment, who sees within and without, and on all sides, only the translucent forms of a single divine energy which is everlasting love and delight, as which and from which he effortlessly radiates peace, charity, and joy. What an enviable situation! We, too, would like to be one of those, but as we start to meditate and look into our-*

selves we find mostly a quaking and palpitating mess of anxiety which lusts and loathes, needs love and attention, and lives in terror of death putting an end to its misery. So we despise that mess, and look for ways of controlling it and putting "how the true mystic feels" in its place, not realizing that this ambition is simply one of the lusts of the quaking mess, and that this, in turn, is a natural form of the universe like rain and frost, slugs and snails, flies and disease. When the "true mystic" sees flies and disease as translucent forms of the divine, that does not abolish them. I—making no hard-and-fast distinction between inner and outer experience—see my quaking mess as a form of the divine, and that doesn't abolish it either. But at least I can live with it.[23]

I watch myself judge my life against Watts's life, and mine is laughably mundane and limited. What are the limits I opted to believe in this life, and how to unlock them? Maybe I should take my tip from his story, lean into joie de vivre. And primary to everything, let go of the desire to transcend.

Watts's story was predominant in my mind leading up to my ordination as a minister in the Church of the Sacred Stream, where I had been trained as a spiritual counselor. As I read his autobiography, I was carried away by the desire for the same ravenous intellectual and internal discovery that marked Watts's life, as well as the hunger for the kind of social life that looks like a who's who of great personalities of the last century. All the while, I was in contemplation about what it means to be in a position to guide people to their own spiritual understanding.

Reading Watts was helpful, as I recognized that I had been struggling to understand the different aspects of my life, contemplative pursuits alongside the shenanigans of a rock-and-roll drummer. Again, I return to the battle of manifestation and spirit.

What does a holy life look like, anyway?

The modern model of a spiritual teacher is one of an elevated physical demeanor. This makes sense, because we have been lulled into believing that spirituality is an aspect of self-help. Through this window, I will always fail to support the proper image. I don't have the kind of yogic discipline you find in this kind of path. I do well for a while, then drift into indulgence with food and entertainment. My connection to my body and weight and eating has been a lifetime of exploration and struggle, and I would never say I have finally come to a balance. This conversation with food is ongoing. No one is going to come to me to be inspired to moderation.

In investigating my lifetime of self-attack, overeating, and my love for and identity with some of the great over-indulgers of the world, I have developed a great deal of understanding. The pain of compulsive behavior has led me to the root of the compulsion, through many paths of healing, and ultimately to an understanding of to whom the compulsion rises. I am certainly not a model for your standard recovery story, but I do have a gift for the path.

I am happy, however, pretty nearly consistently happy. This after years of suffering many dark, internal conflagrations I felt defined by. When I remember the slow progress to put out these fires and the work and time required, I feel I do have something to offer folks who seek my counseling.

Most importantly, I am fearless in my investigation of the concepts that keep me from knowing the divine, keep me from knowing myself as worthy of God love, love that loves without boundary. Nothing can hold me back from living my truth as is aligned with my own lighted way. This is integrity. Like that groove in the mud that makes the gallop happen in a rock song. When you find it, all limits break loose, and there is no getting out.

93 I enter a space on the second floor of an office building. The room is carpeted and bare, with some folding chairs in rows and nothing else. About twenty people have shown up for the past-life regression. We go around the room and people ask questions and say what they expect. One young woman says she wants to know in which life she belongs. She doesn't think she is in the right place in time. She is ready for this life to be over and get on to the next. I am a little surprised the moderator does not seem startled by this blatantly suicidal statement, but maybe she recognizes it as bluster and suffering.

We get comfortable and close our eyes. A long series of hypnotic relaxation exercises unfolds. The first life we see will be our most spiritual life. I follow along, deeper relaxed, forgetting the room around me and the people nearby. I step out of a window into the past. Part of my mind senses I am going through the motions, but I do see the window, so I step.

I am in a field, in the middle of the night. There is bright moonlight around me. My body is firm and round, naked under a linen-type fabric. I gather plants, leaning down and collecting. I feel peaceful. I enter a tent where a fire burns and a young girl is laid out on a raised platform. I am heartbroken when I see her. I feel there is not a family connection, that she is perhaps an apprentice, but I feel great affection. I step aside and grind up the plants I have collected, and go about anointing the girl, on her forehead, on her throat, down her body. When I am finished, I am wracked with sorrow.

I step outside the tent, bereft. I tilt my head to the moonlit sky. I see a star. It grows bigger until bright white light fills my eyes, and a ball speeds down in an instant, a shooting star, aimed for me. It enters the top of my head, and as it radiates down I am filled with a feeling of love and joy, beyond any earthly feeling. Time stands still as my self drops away and I am washed in love, a love so expansive and yet so personal, so tender. When the light reaches my feet it bounces back up, flying up through my body as if I have just been checked off. As the light ascends, I feel the girl's spirit and her love for me. I know I have helped her spirit to leave through the pathways I marked with the anointing. I know this all in an instant.

Years later, I am riding the hour from the Dallas Greyhound station to a meditation center with a stranger, a man who is attending the retreat as well. He seems in his early sixties, very straitlaced and business-y, but with a soft core I intuit. He had manufactured ammunition for the government for a living. How did he come to find Vipassana? I ask.

At the bedside of his dying father, he leaned over to kiss his father on the forehead. As his lips touched the skin, a light shot into him, filling him up with the joy and love of the universe, a feeling beyond any earthly feeling. The light flowed to his feet, filled him up with a love encompassing all love, then left from the top of him, checked him off. He recognized this as his father's spirit entering and leaving his body. He decided it was time to investigate some other ways of being in the world.

94 It occurred to me I don't think I am afraid of death anymore. I had that thought, and then I immediately threw that thought away. How could I possibly live without the fear every person walks in, that defining piece of the human condition? Why did I think I was special?

My neighbor was ill, a wonderful, funny, open, vibrant, kind, spectacular human being. I asked to see her, and I traveled to the hospital. As I was driving I thought, okay, here you go. You will be face-to-face with the sorrow and tragedy of a person dying too young. The grief of the family. The fear of the unknown. Your mistaken idea of a lack of fear of death is not realistic, is actually an insult to those grieving.

I stepped into the room and saw Nancy there, looking so small in the hospital bed. A feeling filled me that was overwhelming, and I fought back tears. Not tears of sorrow but tears at the realization she would be the one to prove this dizzying absence of fear.

I was overwhelmed with the joy that met me when I walked into the room. I cry now when I think of losing her. I feel the grief of her family who lost such a light so young. I remember how sad she was when she finally knew it was the end, and there was so much more to do. It breaks my human heart. But these feelings are not as deep as this truly peaceful one: Nancy is in bliss. She was a joyful and light person in life. In her leaving, she gave to me the gift of proof of our eternal spark.

"Put your awareness in your heart" was my mentor's first instruction, and I imagined placing my eyeballs in the center of my chest and looking out on the moving highway over the dashboard. Over some time, with her patient guidance, I came to recognize that the heart is the expanded knowledge of myself as consciousness, true self. The energy of heart has deepened and expanded until the inner voice of the mind has less and less power. I didn't change the voice. I changed my relationship to it. All the while, the unchanging energy of the One, the unity of all, made itself known.

When we connect with this true energy, it often feels like a recognition rather than surprise. This is why I have come to like the term "realized" rather than "awakened." We realize something we have felt or sensed at different extreme moments in our life. Maybe we first realized it in a time of trauma, when somehow we moved from point A to point B, even with our minds stilled with shock. Maybe we fell into it in reverie, or in the light of creation. I feel it when I am in the song, my body pounding patterns into vibration and my mind perfectly silent. This energy propels us yet feels motionless.

For quite a long time, I was seeing my personality self, the ego and thoughts and emotions, as separate from this center. It has become clear that it is, all of it, the same thing. The pudgy belly and the wrinkles and the irritating foot pain and the negative thoughts, as well as the unconditional love, it all gets equal billing in grace. In thinking they were two different things, ego and true self, I was slipping into what they call spiritual bypassing, which is to preference the absolute over the relative. Spirit over form.

There is danger when we experience the unconditional field, for we suddenly have the ability to avoid feeling pain. We watch our reactions to physical pain or emotional pain, but we don't allow the actual feelings to touch us. Everything becomes light and even-keeled but seen through a veil of avoidance. We become numb to the difficult things.

Blanking out experience is not the point. The point is to feel fully, to live fully, while always retaining equanimity, this field of the unconditional as our guide.

My internal life is like a sky through which rise clouds of frustration, anger, sadness, giddiness, despair, delight, but these things form and are felt and then drift away. Oceans of physical pain stay for a while, then even these are released eventually, and so too the deepest emotions. I am overcome by grief or joy in an instant. I recognize this quality in some people in my life who seem to be similarly realized: tears come quickly and leave just as quickly. It has become commonplace to regularly weep in empathetic feeling publicly for two minutes and not give a damn.

I remember the Old Man's grandmother, how at the end of her one hundred years, her emotions seemed to rise and leave in moments. She would remember her son and weep with grief and two minutes later be laughing at something else.

When we don't attach anything to emotions, adding no story or implication, how long do they stay? I have heard ninety seconds, and this feels consistent with my own experience of grief or nostalgia.

The reason emotions stay is because I get in the way. I feel grief, then I feel a clutching desire for the grief to stay as intensely as it first appeared. So I retell myself a story of the grief, to make it stay. For if it doesn't stay long, then I can't identify as one who is truly grieving.

Sirriya has a simpler way to it all, and I find myself always returning to her teachings. She speaks in the plainest language possible about these things.

Fall into the heart, and know. Allow what rises to rise, stay a while, and then go.

Only when you live from your essence does your life become like music being played by the heavens. It is in harmony and carried by the universal intelligence. Welcome to your song.

~Sirriya Din

The one thing I very much stayed away from over the years was anything to do with God. The concept of the Father in the sky burned out for me very early in my Catholic education. Growing up in Moral Majority country while I was reading Kerouac and Vonnegut, I couldn't get down with the whole thing. It seemed like magical thinking to imagine a being with a big plan.

As the good materialist American I was, I set my mind to agnosticism and went searching for ways to become The Best Clem I Can Be, and in doing that, imagined myself on some kind of path of wisdom and what I called spirituality.

Of course, this idea of creating some higher version of the self only causes misery. When I work to improve the small self, the ego Clem, there is a ceiling there. I am only improving myself to be of better use to the material world: attractive, with a strong work ethic, a striving intelligence. When I go about things this way, there is no way to be enough. There is no way to succeed ultimately. I am forever grasping for more and fighting decay. Happiness comes from things, then those things get taken away. I judge myself against a standard that is always shifting. There is always someone with more.

Even on this path of "wisdom," I work harder and harder, then one day I walk into a library, or I meet someone further along, and a sinking defeat pulls me down. I can never know enough. I can never be enough. The small self is programmed to judge and find lack.

Luckily, fortuitously, I happened upon a way out. I first learned how to hear my internal voice, my thoughts, as separate. Once I distanced myself from my thoughts, I realized those aren't me. I was gifted with my mentor, who taught me to stop identifying with my reactions to the world. I witnessed heavy emotions pass through like storms, and leave, once I invited them to make themselves known. Fear, shame, rage, happiness, grief, I learned to let go of their stories and started to see, *Ah, I get to let go of the fight.* Let go of judgment. Let go of avoiding. Let go of identity. That's not me. Just be.

One day, I lay on the carpet and said, *What is it to die?* I imagined the breath slowing, the warmth fading away, the heart stopping, the spirit uncaged. I witnessed how the terror of this eventuality had shadowed my whole life.

I realized that I said spirit, uncaged.

What is that spirit? Is that who is listening to the thoughts and not reacting to them? Is that who is feeling these emotions, watching them contract the body and then release? Is that who watches the small self and all its limitations? Is something complete here already?

I was agnostic because I needed proof. I didn't like the implications and metaphors. But here, as the small self loses its importance, suddenly I touch the infinite. I experience the singularity of all things. I still cringe at the word, but somehow, a profound knowing flows through me.

In *Autobiography of a Yogi*,[24] there are so many wonderfully mystical, magical stories. Gurus don't eat for decades or manifest to tell someone they are taking a later train. There are levitations and secret messages from beyond the grave. Listening to the book during a weekend of shows, I live in Yogananda's reality, in which these things are possible. I let my imagination run away a little.

Before my show one night, rather than doing stick exercises, I lie down and see if I can bring the deathless guru Babaji into my heart. I ask him for a well-played show, to rain down love and connection on all the beings in the building. A dream of lotus petals falling into my upturned hands passes through my mind's eye, and I rise refreshed and a little giddy.

Psychologist Tara Brach told a story of a teacher standing over a child in a classroom. The child says she is drawing a picture of God, and the teacher tells the child that no one knows what God looks like.

"They will now!" the child says without missing a beat.

All my life I scoffed at certainty. Maybe I will always cringe when I say the word God. My mentor says she finds the word Consciousness suits her better. I like that too. I like to think of the energy that existed before form, before matter, before the big bang, this creative energy looking for something to do. When I let go of language and am truthful in myself, I see what it is I have been discovering. I must acknowledge this tangible experience, what feels like proof.

I guess I am not agnostic anymore.

As I play drums, sound waves crash through light waves and love falls like lotus petals. This manifest body communes with energy while the spirit stays still. In the center is an infinite blossoming truth. So really, who am I kidding?

97 There is a baby in the seat before me here on the airplane, and for some time now we have gazed steadfastly into each other's eyes, each cooing in the connection. The blue of her eyes is so intent and gorgeous tears stream from mine. There I go again.

I look out the window, and the clouds there are so luscious and rosy that if we were to plummet through them to the field below, I have to believe I might not even mind. This is what it is like to trust in my knowing, in the depth and joy stitching the fabric of reality. More and more, fear falls away.

I delight both in this expanded view and in yet another airplane ride, yet another rock show, yet another family obligation, yet another normal moment. I want to be here, really here, every moment possible. I will leave myself to dive another day.

I have come to believe that we are here solely to experience. Maybe I will never again be able to let go of the searching long enough to allow the window of oneness to open as it did in that first meditation retreat or in light of that first taste of flower. I can do nothing but what I am called in truth to do. I have faith I will get to experience the light again, even if it is not until the end, when Clem turns to light herself and all is singing.

During [Rabbi Herschel Lymon]'s reentry from his LSD session, in which he experienced a shattering encounter with death and subsequent feeling of spiritual rebirth, he remembered a famous statement made five hundred years ago by Leonardo da Vinci. At the time when he was dying, Leonardo summarized his feelings about his rich and productive life by saying, "I thought I was living; I was only preparing myself to die." Rabbi Lymon, describing the death-rebirth struggle in his LSD session, paraphrased Leonardo's words: "I thought I was dying; I was only preparing myself to live."

~Stanislav Grof and Joan Halifax [25]
The Human Encounter with Death

98

I had a dream I was a dog. I was aware as I was walking around that I was in a kind of ecstasy most of the time, but there were moments when I was angry and barking. I was speaking to someone and saying, *I'm a dog because I came back here to work out the last of this futile anger. I'm here to release this last bit of worldly emotion.*

I am not sure why I gravitate toward the idea of reincarnation. Intellectually, it seems a little too neat of a situation, that we keep coming back in order to educate the soul until the day comes when we clear out all the baggage and let go the sankharas that hold us back from enlightenment, so we don't have to return anymore.

As a young child, I would have dreams of grown-up situations, streets that had no place in my reality, worlds that a four-year-old with limited television access could not have invented. There were strangely familiar urban environments, clearly furnished rooms, characters and situations populating my reality. I don't know where they came from.

Back then, I was a bad sleeper. I would wake in the night and walk through the house, making sure nothing was on fire, nobody had died. I was worried and afraid of the dark. I am still afraid of the dark. I spook easily, and when I am home alone the lights in the house are blazing.

When I was very young, I developed a technique to help myself sleep I have used throughout my life. I would start at the top of my head and try to relax every part of my body all the way down, noticing every bit, trying to feel it in my mind, often not making it all the way to the feet before I would fall asleep.

At my first Vipassana retreat, when they taught us this exact same technique over the course of ten days, I recognized it as something I was born knowing.

We are each a map of living bacteria, some of which can attach to our DNA and, in a sense, travel through time. Maybe these things I knew as a child were cellular memories of my ancestors, bacteria releasing my great grandparents' experiences into my consciousness.

In my first past-life regression, the one we might call "past-life tourism,"[26] the two lives I experienced were of a Native American woman and a Scandinavian man. I have both ethnicities in my immediate family history. Maybe when I was dreaming these supposed "past lives," it was my bacteria remembering, firing off old memories through the dark channels of my biology.

From the time I was a child, I have had ecstatic experiences of being bathed in a feeling of pure happiness. Intellectually, I see these moments as an imbalance of chemicals and hormones in my body. Maybe my face was buried in the pillow, and I was sleeping so deeply it was triggering an experience of oxygen deprivation. Maybe I was overtired, and my neurotransmitters released some chemicals to soothe me. Maybe I am a bag of muscle and potion, and the balance is fraught with happenstance and coincidence. Maybe my search for enlightenment is being generated in my temporal lobe, and it is all just chemistry.

In the twilight of my mind as I woke from the dog dream, the idea of reincarnation was again around me. I saw my life from a distance. I asked, If I am an infinite being, why did I come to this planet as a suburban middle-class Californian, blandly following her passion for music in a tribute band, happy in love, happy in life, never too much of anything? Moments of oneness, moments of no-self, but then always coming back to live this very simple and relatively uneventful life?

Here I am with the sum of my years, being born and my family and schooling and friends and career and income and struggles and sorrows and passions and emotions, and it occurs to me I am exactly as capable of knowing the divine as the guru on the mountain with the matted hair and the beatific expression. I don't need to do anything to be it. I am it.

I see myself in my childhood bedroom, the small boxy room with the cleanly painted walls and the carpeting and the light through the white blinds and the dresser painted blue, the drone of a lawn mower outside the window and my family somewhere. A little body in a box on a planet spinning through the solar system and the galaxy, floating in millions of years of time, and I am as enlightened then as now.

Underneath this personality, underneath my mind and all my intellectual volleyball, is awareness that animates all my reality. I am the dark matter and dark energy, and the entire biome of the universe rests in me. I am here to learn that it doesn't matter, the face of it. I am the love of the universe. It doesn't matter what I think is happening, reincarnation or dust to dust. It doesn't matter if this is the only time or one of a thousand times I am to be here. I contain it all.

When I remember, I will take a breath. I will watch it travel from my head to my feet, sink beneath this Clementine personality who has been set here for some undisclosed reason or purely by accident. I will expand into the knowing that we are all divine, that we are each walking infinity. Even this corny Southern California suburban-born tribute band drummer.

99 An outdoor festival, after the set. I am
standing by the van amid my drums,
relaxing a little before the dismantling
begins. A man and a woman walk over with their three- or
four-year-old son.

"He couldn't take his eyes off you the whole time. We think
drums are his favorite." The little boy stands next to dad's pant
leg, quietly staring at me. As I talk to his parents, I drag the
drum seat and floor tom over, adjust them to his height, then
pat the seat. "Come on up, dude, you want to play?"

He scrambles up on the seat, and I hand him a stick.

"Put your hand out. Here's how you hold it. Turn your
hand over like this and slide the stick in there. Okay, go ahead,
hit the drum."

He looks at his parents and then sideways at me. He taps
the drum.

I smile.

"No, HIT it!" THWACK.

The little boy jumps at the sound. An electric smile spreads
over his face. Staring me right in the eye, he lifts the stick slowly and WHAM!

He giggles as his parents snap back with the sound.

"Good!" I hand him another stick, and he starts to go to
town on the drum as I pack up. His parents are delighted.
"Now you've done it!"

A few hours later, I am wandering the festival, and I see the
family come running over to me. The little boy is still gripping
the sticks I had given him.

"He wants to tell you something," they say.

"Hi, dude, what's up?"

He's shy again. "He wants to tell you that he has a set of drums."

I kneel down. "Wow, you have some drums at home? Well, you know what to do with them, right?"

That grin spreads like lightning across his face. He looks me straight in the eye, shyness gone, and WHAM, hits the dirt with a powerful thud and adds that little giggle afterward.

There is such a beauty in LOUD. In making yourself heard. Command the eardrums, command attention. My life before drums was spent trying to crawl back into myself to be invisible, to be quiet, to be unnoticed. But glorious sound released me.

Right now as you're reading this, WHOOP! out into the still air, clap your hands, make a noise, make yourself heard, and hear the repercussions. Sound splashes into silence like a stone dropping into water. It ripples out, and silence smooths over the place where the noise just was. We are here, with the whole universe listening. Our songs tumble like rain into the river of time.

100

I would like to offer a remedy to all ills.

Play more drums.

This has become my answer to anything that ails me. Headache? Grouchiness? Financial anxiety? Pain somewhere? Family morass?

Play More Drums.

Drumming fixes everything. No, really, it fixes EVERYTHING.

I am a pretty light person. I keep it pretty chipper. That said, I battle darkness from time to time, certainly. I am fortunate to have a partner who can see when my outlook begins to turn grim, often even before I notice.

I am also very lucky that the Old Man happens to have a green, sparkly John Bonham–reissue drum kit sitting in storage. He could see the tides turning in my mind as we visited family in the Midwest, so we grabbed the drums from the locker, set them up.

I then passed a glorious few hours in which everything got better.

The room I played in has soundproofing on the walls. The kit sounded so warm and luscious I started secretly plotting to wheedle it from the Old Man one of these days. For the moment, my cure for all that ails me was right here.

Play More Drums.

If I don't play for a while and then sit down, sometimes I will come away from practicing with a sore wrist or ankle. The cure?

Play More Drums.

If I overexert myself exercising, I take the following day off, give the muscles a rest. Not with drums. Wrist a little sore from drumming? Make sure and play the next day, and it will be magically cured.

My body just wants to play drums. It will give me a little grief as punishment for taking time off, but as long as I make practice happen the following day, I am making a deal with the drums to fix what ails me. It is magic.

With the green drums, I ran through Zeppelin songs and then decided to goof around and learn "Tom Sawyer." I never tried to play a Rush song, and it was ridiculously fun. The Old Man's response to family stress seems to be Listen To More Rush, so I had been hearing a lot of it driving around Omaha. It occurred to me that it would be a good idea to learn some Neil Peart licks (apparently, I am laughably obtuse about certain obvious ideas others take for granted).

Anyway, I came upstairs and attitude, adjusted. Heart, open. Misery and darkness, set to the wind. Why do I always allow myself to forget?

I see realization as remembering to remember. In each moment, there is the potential to know myself as infinite. If I could just remember this, all the time, how life would be.

And if I could remember to Play More Drums, I wouldn't have to sink down, get sad and worried and live with all the mental baloney that meets me when dealing with challenges of daily life. If I remembered to remember, how simple my state, no matter these illusions of moments.

Drums were love at first sight. When I play, it is an expression of love, love of communication and sound and movement and connection. Vibration and resonance and frequency and sound waves and eardrums and heartbeats. Drums call me and use me to their will. They offer truth in motion.

To that field of consciousness that brought music to me, drumming to me, I send this frequency of gratitude. Open each chamber in my heart with your beating, I ask, until there is no wall left.

EPILOGUE

The last show I played before the pandemic was at the end of February, at a rock venue in Orlando. The band had been trying for years to get to Florida, a state packed with promoters notorious for not wanting to pay artists enough to get them there. I returned home in celebration and watched as the itinerary fell away for the rest of the year in the wake of the illness.

It was an adjustment to change gears after almost thirty years of constant travel. The first thing I noticed was that I was tired. The driving and flying and loading and late nights had created a vein of fatigue I had not taken time to notice. Sleep became a priority. Then, an enjoyment of routine rose in me, that often dreamed-of state of regularity impossible in a life of constant movement.

I tapped out stick exercises now and then on the electronic drum kit crammed into my small San Francisco apartment, but drums faded as priority for a while. I devoted myself to spiritual practice and study, reading, writing. I concentrated on silent things. Even the ringing in my ears seemed to quiet down.

In a relationship of twenty years between two people touring with bands, 2020 became the most sustained time of daily living the Old Man and I had ever spent together. We saw no one for months, except neighbors on walks, and on furtive trips to the grocery store. Lucky for us, we realized we liked each other, even without the fuel of constant goodbyes and reunions that had built our years. I suspected that Henry the pug had devised the whole global catastrophe in order to have us all to himself. We lived as Henry would like us to: routine, ample cookies, and couch time built into each day.

The desire for the sound of guitar cabinets in my ears was the first longing, which came in a big whoosh as I walked through the quiet San Francisco streets one afternoon. A few days later, the desire to be onstage with people I love ached through me, as I remembered the intuitive synchronicity of playing music with other people. I began to fantasize about the musty smell of theaters, the ocean of volume piping through the space, and the magic energy of sound moving bodies and vibrating through molecules.

I was being called to the drums. When I made it back, they met me as if I had never left. I was amazed I hadn't lost any memory of songs, and the techniques of my feet and hands didn't seem to have lagged much. To play felt as joyful as ever. It was as if the drums knew I needed some rest, and they were there to meet me in anticipation of what was to come when I was ready. I arrived properly devotional.

This writing kept me company for two years, and I recognized in these pages the affirmation of how unifying a rock concert can be, how much healing music provides. I watched as the world suffered and divided itself without that connection.

Sound travels through one body and into another and another. Who knows what a song carries with it as it flows. Getting back to this seems vitally important, as without it, society seems in danger of forgetting our common heart.

With the dearest prayer for peace and unity,
Clementine Moss, June 2022

In Gratitude

This book would not have happened without the wisdom and brilliant coaching of Genine Lentine. It was copyedited by the marvelous Shawna Hampton of Magic Words Editorial Services. The cover was created by the fantastic artist Geoff Peveto, who continued the inspired work he began with posters for BOTTOM all those years ago. It was laid out by wonderful Tamian Wood of Beyond Design Books, and the e-book adapted by Kimberly Hitchens of Booknook.biz. Finally, it came into physical manifestation by the generosity of my dear friend Amara Palmer.

My beautiful and magical family: my mother Daria and marvelous Jack Clement, Daphne, Jon, Madison, Mackensie Peace and Roman Manning, and Jessica, Jason, Deacon and Duke Whelchel. It is impossible to relate how your love has sustained me, a base from which all journeys began.

My dear friends who are also family: Jeannine and Preston Prince, Nila Minnerup, Gretchen Menn, Elizabeth Cahill. The Omaha crew: Jerry and Julie Hug, Trey and Lallaya Lalley, Lee and Tricia Meyerpeter, and John and Jenny Wolf. Thank you for putting up with all my bad behavior and for adding so much sparkle to my life.

My marvelous friend and booking agent Mary Goree, who is magic. My dear friends and bandmates who are also family: Anna Kristina, Holly West, Justin Caucutt, Daniele Gottardo, Nili Brosh, and so many others I cannot list them for fear of forgetting someone with my rock-addled brain. Just know if we played music together, I have loved connecting with you in that magical conversation.

Robert Preston, thank you not only for enabling me in creating music but also for always reminding me of the absolutely joyful party that is life. And Mahoko Kuramasu, thank you for keeping him in line and for your inspired contribution to the band's video presence.

My wonderful friends and colleagues Dina Varano, Erica Smigielski, Cyn Herr, Katie Healey, and Sarah Hylton, light beings Helen Kramer, Rudy Hunter, and George Koury, as well as all the wonderful practitioners and clients who have trusted me to enter their journey.

My teachers, these remarkable gifts to whom I am forever indebted. To the dream that is Sirriya Din, we are forever together in the heart. Isa Gucciardi and Laura Chandler and The Foundation of the Sacred Stream, you have revealed vistas. Ishtar Howell, you are an unexpected bonus of delight. S. N. Goenka. Terri Iacuzzo. Jabeen Jaferrji. Paul Selig and his guides.

Fred Klatz, the Best Drum Teacher in New York City, thank you for the lifelong friendship and for showing me the way. Thank you to all the drummers who have offered so much inspiration and information, and to the drum teachers and vocal coaches who helped, and help, me hone the craft of music.

A great thank you to friends and guides who helped with my writing: Jeannine Prince, Kay Franklin, Dina Varano, and Simone Kaplan. How lucky to have folks much wiser than me to trust.

Much love to my dear mother-in-law Donna Hulsebus-Moss, the most glamorous woman in Omaha, Nebraska.

I hold so much appreciation for my Patreon contributors, the Zepparella Zoom Posse, all the audiences and fellow musicians, and each person who has contributed to my music career. I could never tell you how dearly I love meeting our single heart through a rock concert.

And finally, a deep transmission of love to the Old Man, Tim Moss, who has grounded me, and in so doing, enabled me to fly. And to Henry Badass Kissinger, pug extraordinaire, for ensuring I will never forget how to love.

BIBLIOGRAPHY

Evans, Barry. "Myth of the Invisible Ships." *North Coast Journal*, July 23, 2009.

Grof, Stanislav and Halifax, Joan. *The Human Encounter with Death*. New York: E. P. Dutton, 1977.

Howard, Vernon. "The pain of ego, letting go, noticing thoughts, self-realization, & mindfulness." External Perception. YouTube video, 14:26. https://youtu.be/41qA91w9QFo.

Jones, Peter C. and Elena Mannes, dir. *A Rising Tide of Silence*. Syndicado, 2015. http://www.fatherthomaskeating.com.

Moss, Clementine. "On Channeling John Bonham in 12 Steps." *On the Beat* (blog), *Modern Drummer*, June 2020. https://www.moderndrummer.com/2020/06/clementine-on-channeling-john-bonham-in-12-steps/.

Oliver, Mary. "The Mockingbirds." *The Atlantic* 273, no. 2 (February 1994): 80.

Poncelet, Claude. *The Shaman Within*, Boulder, Colorado: Sounds True, 2014.

Rilke, Rainer Maria. "For the Sake of a Single Poem." In *The Selected Poetry of Rainer Maria Rilke,* translated by Stephen Mitchell. New York: Random House, 1982.

Rilke, Rainer Maria. *Letters to a Young Poet*. Rev. ed. New York: W. W. Norton, 1993.

Thoreau, Henry David. *Walden; or, Life in the Woods*. New York: Penguin, 1999.

Tippett, Krista. "Alice Parker: Singing Is the Most Companionable of Arts." *On Being with Krista Tippett*, December 6, 2016. Podcast, 50:59.

Tippett, Krista. "Brian Greene: Reimagining the Cosmos." *On Being with Krista Tippett*, June 1, 2017. Podcast, 51:46.

Tolle, Ekhart. *The Power of Now: A Guide to Spiritual Enlightenment.* Novato, CA: New World Publishing, 1999.

Watts, Alan. *In My Own Way.* New York: Pantheon Books, 1972.

Yogananda, Paramahansa. *Autobiography of a Yogi.* 12th ed. Los Angeles: Self-Realization Fellowship, 1994.

End Notes

[1]. Eckart Tolle, *The Power of Now: A Guide to Spiritual Enlightenment* (Novato, CA: New World Publishing, 1999), 48.

[2]. Sirriya Din, *http://www.morphicawakening.com*.

[3]. Henry David Thoreau, *Walden; or, Life in the Woods* (New York: Penguin Group, 1999), 258. "I love to see that Nature is so rife with life that myriads can be afforded to be sacrificed and suffered to prey on one another; that tender organizations can be so serenely squashed out of existence like pulp—tadpoles which herons gobble up, and tortoises and toads run over in the road; and that sometimes it has rained flesh and blood! With the liability to accident, we must see how little account is to be made of it. The impression made on a wise man is that of universal innocence."

[4]. "Quantum superposition," Wikimedia Foundation, last modified July 19, 2022, 13:52, https://en.wikipedia.org/wiki/Quantum_superposition.

[5]. Barry Evans, "Myth of the Invisible Ships," North Coast Journal, July 23, 2009, https://www.northcoastjournal.com/humboldt/myth-of-the-invisible-ships/Content?oid=2129921. This story was recanted in the movie *What The Bleep Do We Know!?* and has since been refuted in several places, like here.

[6]. Clementine Moss, "On Channeling John Bonham in 12 Steps," *On the Beat* (blog), *Modern Drummer,* June 2020, https://www.moderndrummer.com/2020/06/clementine-on-channeling-john-bonham-in-12-steps.

[7]. Rainer Maria Rilke, "For the Sake of a Single Poem," in *The Selected Poetry of Rainer Maria Rilke,* trans. Stephen Mitchell (New York: Random House, 1982).

[8]. Alan Watts, *In My Own Way* (New York: Pantheon Books, 1972), 125.

[9]. Nishida, T., "bonobo," Encyclopedia Britannica, June 26, 2021, https://www.britannica.com/animal/bonobo.

[10]. Duncan Trussell, *The Duncan Trussell Family Hour,* podcast, https://podcasts.apple.com/us/podcast/duncan-trussell-family-hour/id350580455.

[11]. "Brahmavihara," Wikimedia Foundation, last modified July 13, 2022, 10:48, https://en.wikipedia.org/wiki/Brahmavihara.

[12] Ramana Maharshi.

[13]. Rainer Maria Rilke, *Letters to a Young Poet,* rev. ed. (New York: W. W. Norton, 1993). "Love consists of this: two solitudes that meet, protect and greet each other."

[14]. Vernon Howard, "The pain of ego, letting go, noticing thoughts, self-realization, & mindfulness," External Perception, YouTube video, 14:26, https://youtu.be/41qA91w9QFo.

[15]. Krista Tippett, "Brian Greene: Reimagining the Cosmos," June 1, 2017, in *On Being with Krista Tippett,* podcast, 51:46, https://onbeing.org/programs/brian-greene-reimagining-the-cosmos.

[16]. Paul Selig, https://paulselig.com. These concepts are inspired by channelings by Paul Selig.

[17]. *A Rising Tide of Silence*, directed by Peter C. Jones and Elena Mannes (Syndicado, 2015), http://www.fatherthomaskeating.com.

[18]. Krista Tippett, "Alice Parker: Singing Is the Most Companionable of Arts," December 6, 2016, in *On Being with Krista Tippett*, podcast, 50:59, https://onbeing.org/programs/alice-parker-singing-is-the-most-companionable-of-arts.

[19]. "Kalapa (atomism)," Wikimedia Foundation, last modified April 20, 2021, 16:48, https://en.wikipedia.org/wiki/Kalapas. In Theravada Buddhist phenomenology, Kalapas are defined as the smallest units of physical matter. Kalapas are described as tiny units of materiality, "tens of thousands of times smaller than a particle of dust," coming into existence and disappearing in as little as a billionth of a second or a trillionth of the blink of an eye. Kalapas are understood by some Therevada thinkers as actual subatomic particles and the smallest units of materiality.

[20]. Shea Slemmer, http://www.sheaslemmer.com.

[21]. Mary Oliver, "The Mockingbirds," *The Atlantic* 273, no. 2 (February 1994): 80.

[22]. Claude Poncelet, *The Shaman Within*, (Boulder, Colorado: Sounds True, 2014):

[23]. Watts, *In My Own Way*, 211.

[24]. Paramahansa Yogananda, *Autobiography of a Yogi*, 12th ed. (Los Angeles: Self-Realization Fellowship, 1994).

[25]. Stanislav Grof and Joan Halifax, *The Human Encounter with Death*, (New York: E. P. Dutton, 1977), 221.

[26]. I am making a distinction between this sort of regression, in which we were to go back to see our most spiritual life and our most recent life, and the sort of regressions I do as a Depth Hypnosis Practitioner, in which we are following patterns in this life to discover their origin. The purpose in Depth Hypnosis is not more story but to release suffering.

ABOUT THE AUTHOR

CLEMENTINE MOSS is the founder and drummer of Zepparella, with a busy solo career as a singer and songwriter. A graduate of UC Santa Cruz with a creative writing degree, her writing path gave way to a musical one until she began her blog *Bliss and Drumming* in 2016. In the essays, tales of her music career provide metaphor for contemplative practice, and many of those pieces are found in various forms in, and were the impetus for, this book.

Clementine is a spiritual counselor and a nondenominational Minister at The Foundation for the Sacred Stream. Using the modalities of Depth Hypnosis, Applied Shamanism, Energy Medicine, Sound Healing, and Morphic Awakening techniques, Clem has an active healing practice. She is certified in Contemplative Psychotherapy and Conflict Resolution. A Vipassana meditator for over thirty years, her study and personal practice spans many traditions.

She lives in San Francisco with music manager and musician Tim Moss, and Henry the pug. Her writing has appeared in *Modern Drummer Magazine, Memoir Magazine,* and several other online publications. Her children's book, written with Sirriya Din, *Shiva and The Song of the Heart,* will be released in 2023.

ClemtheGreat.com

Photo credit: Shannon Corr

Lightning Source UK Ltd.
Milton Keynes UK
UKHW042307150223
417099UK00029B/330/J

.